Beyond
The Da Vinci Code

CONTENTS

INTRODUCTION

INTRODUCTION

Once every so often a book appears that challenges some of society's very foundations. It may be a work of fiction or an essay; one or several authors may have written it; it may turn out to be a bestseller or, on the contrary, be purchased and read by only a small number of readers. The potential variants are, obviously, many. Nonetheless, the fact is that this type of text bursts into society generating controversy, polemic and debate; as a result, it is attacked by some and defended by others.

This revolutionary capacity is not, of course, reserved exclusively to books, but can extend (and in fact, it does) to film, music, painting, plays and other cultural products.

In all instances, these are works that uncover a breach, a gap, an opening within matters which that period's culture considered to be resolved, closed to debate, unquestionable. These controversial texts interrogate what a society had supposed, up until that moment, an undeniable truth.

This is the case with *The Da Vinci Code*, which has been described as 'a sort of esoteric thriller featuring attacks on Catholicism' and as 'a compendium of worn and ridiculous esoteric and Gnostic theories'. It has even been claimed that 'hate against Catholicism permeates the whole book'. Furthermore, Brown's novel has been accused of championing an extremist feminist perspective, while it has also been pointed out that the author's work is credible, yet dishonest.

Yet, of course, *The Da Vinci Code* has not solely received negative criticism. It has also been acclaimed as 'an intelligent thriller that, without a doubt, can be recommended with resounding enthusiasm', and it has been stated that it is based upon impeccable research. Last, but not least, the book has encouraged a large number of its readers to delve further into the undoubtedly contentious themes treated within its pages. Numerous debate forums can be found on the Internet, where the book's polemical subject-matter is examined. Within these forums, some people wholly agree with Dan Brown's expositions, others are unsure or mildly reticent, while a third group put forward differing beliefs. All in all, people are keen on investigating and discussing the many enigmas presented in the text. Might this surge of popular interest and curiosity be the reason why the book has received so many attacks? Who is being troubled or inconvenienced by the ideas presented in Brown's novel?

Let us now turn to the specific; what exactly does *The Da Vinci Code* talk about, and why has it provoked such a commotion?

Beyond the novel's plot line (an American symbology expert and Harvard professor is invited to attend a conference in Paris, where he arranges to meet one of the Louvre museum's most renowned curators, who is coincidentally murdered that same evening...), it is certain ideas about Christianity divulged in the book that have caused a stir within large parts of society. It is obviously impossible to present all of these ideas within an introduction such as this one, but we may summarize them as follows: Mary Magdalene was Jesus' wife; when he was crucified, Magdalene fled to France escaping persecution; she was pregnant at the time and, in the country that offered her refuge, gave birth to Sarah, her daughter and that of Jesus; their descendants became the Merovingian dynasty; the Vatican has done, and still does, everything in its power to conceal this truth, but the descendants of Christ have had allies from the beginning, specifically in the Knights Templar and the Priory of Sion; the latter being a secret society that dates back centuries, and that continues to act in the present, one of its main objectives being the restitution of power to the Merovingian dynasty.

These are, among others, the ideas and the theory that *The Da Vinci Code* expounds, and which have generated so much disquiet and anxiety. These are also the premises explored in this book. There exists 'another story', an alternative look at the origins and development of Christianity that has been silenced by the Vatican and its powerful allies.

Each reader, both of *The Da Vinci Code* and of this book, is free to believe or not in this alternative account of events. What is impossible though, is to silence the events themselves any longer.

René Chandelle

CHAPTER 1

JESUS IN HIS
TIME

JESUS IN HIS TIME

Who was the real Jesus Christ? Was he the Son of God? Or perhaps just a man with revolutionary tendencies that were highly inconvenient to those in power at the time? Was he a mystic? Maybe a visionary or a prophet? Did he remain celibate or, in accordance to the Judaic norms of the time, did he marry? If the latter is true, did he have any descendants? What role did Mary Magdalene play in his life? The questions could, of course, go on and on. In spite of how much has been written, discussed, reflected upon and filmed regarding Christ, the truth is that, in large part, he is still an enigma; perhaps humanity's greatest mystery.

There is an essential question, the answer to which it is vital to grasp, that must be taken into account when answering our previous queries regarding Jesus and his life: is the image of Jesus Christ portrayed in the Gospels reliable and absolute? The answer is categorical: no. And this answer is precisely the one that allows those with an open mind to investigate more thoroughly, and, at the same time, to comprehend Jesus in more depth.

The official or canonical Gospels, known to us all as the New Testament, allow us to recreate a vision of Jesus Son of God as an exceedingly kind-hearted being, who pitied the suffering of others and who, above all, maintained no sexual contact with women (and consequently, could not have been a husband or father). However, an alternative series of texts and documents offers a different image of Jesus to the one officially maintained by the Catholic Church throughout the centuries. These non-canonical texts are known as the Apocrypha, and there is a multiplicity of them in existence: the Nag Hammadi papyrus codices and the Dead Sea scrolls (also known as the Qumran manuscripts) are among them. But what do all of these writings have in common? Basically, they represent so-called proto-Christianity or early Christianity, before the Roman emperor Constantine (in 325 AD) transformed it into a religion capable of yielding political and financial interests.

The aforementioned Nag Hammadi papyrus codices are considered to be the most important source of information on this alternative portrayal of Jesus hidden by the Church for centuries. All of the above manuscript documents are also known as the Gnostic Gospels or Gnostic Scriptures.

THE GNOSTICS

Before we start talking specifically about the Gnostic Gospels or Scriptures, we need to clarify the following: who were the Gnostics? What image of God did they hold? How did they understand religion?

The Gnostics were a group of primitive Christians who wrote a series of documents – including those now known as the Gnostic Gospels – in search of a higher level of understanding and knowledge (Greek *gnosis*) of things. The birth of this religious practice took place in the Mediterranean region, where the most advanced civilisations of antiquity had settled and flourished (Egyptians, Assyrians, Greeks and Jews).

The term Gnostic means 'possessor of knowledge' and identifies those who have received a secret and wonderful understanding – a 'gnosis' or 'knowledge – from a divine entity. According to the Gnostics, salvation was obtained through possession of this divine knowledge and not through faith, as proclaimed later on by the Church.

The pillars of the Gnostic creed were spiritual and mystical experience. Gnostic believers claimed to be in possession of a divine revelation that led to redemption and that had been transmitted from person to person since the times of Adam (or at least, since the times of his son Seth). To them, the God appearing in the Old Testament represented only a divine agent of a secondary order, a Demiurge. The real God was mysterious and unknown, absolutely transcendental and completely good. This God had not wanted to remain in His infinite peace and solitude and had wished to communicate. This desire to communicate had produced around Him a series of divine projections – or means of contacting the exterior – that had ultimately generated the universe, and humanity with it. Human beings, composed of matter (also created by God) and spirit, could regain their unity with this ineffable and ultra-transcendental God: the Gnostics believed that man was of the same nature as the divine and, because of this, communication between both sides was entirely possible.

The Gnostics were real dissidents in the ancient world: as they rejected matter, nothing stemming from the material world was important to them. This was in stark contrast to other mortals, who feverishly yearned for what the physical world had to offer. In its place, the Gnostics promoted spiritual and intellectual values as a means to returning to Heaven, the original homeland of man and where he would be reunited with God. Although they tried to lead their existence as part of the other Christian groups, they did so maintaining a certain distance, so as to enjoy their divine revelations in a sort of internal voluntary exile. The Gnostics divided humanity into three groups or categories:

• Within the first category, the Gnostics placed themselves: the 'spirituals' or 'immaterials', who had attained 'gnosis' (revelation or knowledge) and would reach salvation if they remained faithful to it.

• In second place were the 'psychics', who had a soul, but were missing a spirit (the divine spark). During their life they acted according to the dictates of a good conscience, but they had not received knowledge of the transcendental or 'gnosis'. When they died, they attained a middle-ground or lesser salvation in a place far from the Earth (a sort of superlunary region that was not fully celestial). The majority of Christians in those times were classified under this category.

• Within the third and last group were the 'hilics' or 'materials', who behaved like animals as they had no soul or spirit. This sector was mainly composed of pagans, who were condemned to the purest form of perdition: at their deaths, all of their substance was doomed to disintegration.

As they rejected the material fully, for the Gnostics original sin consisted in the fact of existing in a flesh-and-blood body. They based their beliefs on what they considered to be the evil nature of the material body and so they conceded no importance to morality. Their acts and conduct went from one extreme to the other, from rigorous asceticism to orgies. Their argument being that what the material body (something base and despicable) did could not be judged or condemned, when what was truly important was the spirit.

THE GNOSTIC GOSPELS

The Gnostic Gospels are a series of difficult-to-interpret texts that were written in Coptic (a popular form of Egyptian writing, successor to the language spoken by the authors of hieroglyphics) between the 3rd and 5th centuries AD. However, the original Greek texts – from which these copies in the Coptic language were made – go back as far as the 1st century AD.

As they offered a different image of primitive Christianity to the one commonly held up until then, the discovery of these texts had a truly revolutionary effect on theology and Christology (the study of God and the study of Christ respectively). During the early centuries of our era, these treatises were considered heretical documents and a sort of sub-product of Christianity, known mostly for its attacks on the early Fathers of the Church. From the 2nd century AD onwards, to be found in possession of these documents became a criminal offence, so they were made to disappear. This is the reason why, from time to time, by chance or by premeditation, Gnostic Gospels are uncovered in the Middle East: they must have been secretly hidden there at the time, in order to save the lives of those who possessed them.

THE NAG HAMMADI CODICES

Up until 1945, little or next to nothing was known about the Gnostics. Apart from a few details, most of the information held about them had its source in the pen of their enemies, which was not flattering or objective in the least. However, when World War Two ended, an Egyptian villager named Muhammad Ali Samman, who was wandering with his camels about Nag Hammadi (the ancient Chenoboskion, in Upper Egypt), found an antique amphora – measuring half a metre in height – within a large lump of sand that had been disturbed by the rain. He immediately imagined the red earthenware jar could contain a treasure that would save him from his difficult existence, and wasted no time in opening it. His disappointment was great when he discovered that the ancient jar contained neither gold nor precious stones, but that it had solely served as protection for several small leather-bound books, half-worn by the passing of time. Despite his understandable disappointment, Muhammed Ali Samman had unknowingly uncovered a treasure far more important to humanity than a thousand amphorae brimming with gold and diamonds: he had found the Nag Hammadi codices, thirteen papyrus books bound in leather, constituting a priceless collection of documents on primitive Christianity and fundamentally of a Gnostic character. Specifically, the Nag Hammadi papyrus manuscripts are the most important source of information on Gnostic beliefs discovered to date. Overall, the thirteen books held about fifty Gnostic works copied into their pages, most of them unknown at that date, and including the fascinating Gospel of Thomas. In this way, the desert sands of Egypt had delivered to historical science a possibility without equal: that of directly studying documents that could shed a new light on the history of the primordial era of Christianity and, in particular, on the evolution of Christianity in Egypt during its early period.

According to investigations carried out with the aid of modern technology, the papyrus books are understood to date back to the end of the 4th century, or beginning of the 5th. Thanks to this research, we also know that the manuscripts found are copies of originals that date even farther back in time. Some of these texts are even mentioned by the first Fathers of the Church (Clement of Alexandria, Irenaeus and Origen), such

THE WONDROUS JOURNEYS OF THE NAG HAMMADI CODICES

What became of the Nag Hammadi papyrus codices once they were unearthed? After discovering them, Muhammad Ali Samman took the books home and dumped them on the straw piled on the ground next to the oven. Samman's mother then burnt many of the papyrus loose pages in the oven, together with the straw laid to kindle the fire. Later on, Samman decided to hand over part of the books to the priest Al-Qummus Basiliyus Abd el Masih. From that moment on, the codices changed hands several times, were sold on the black market and experienced numerous adventures. The three basic itineraries they followed were these:

• The first part of the papyrus books was given to the priest Al-Qummus Basiliyus Abd el Masih, who subsequently sent them on to Raghib, a local historian. In this way, this part of the treasure became the property of the Coptic Museum in Cairo, where it was examined by the French Egyptologist Jean Doresse. After Doresse had examined them and proclaimed the true worth of the discovery, it became clear that it was necessary to find and reunite the rest of the manuscript collection.
• The second part of the codex library fell into the hands of a bandit, Bahij Ali of the Samman village. After it was sold to Phocion Tano, an antiques dealer in Cairo, the Egyptian government tried to purchase it. The dealer informed government officials that the manuscripts had been sold on to an Italian collector living in Cairo, Miss Dattari. In 1952, the Egyptian Ministry of Education declared the manuscripts a national treasure, and so the Dattari codex collection also became part of the Coptic Museum in Cairo.
• The final part of the papyrus codices was also sold on the black market, and purchased by Albert Eid, another Egyptian antiques dealer. In order to avoid having to hand over the codices to the Egyptian government, the dealer smuggled them out of Egypt and offered them for sale in America. Unable to sell the books in America, he then placed them in a security deposit box in Belgium. After his death, Albert Eid's wife continued to try to sell the manuscripts illicitly. Word of the codices soon reached Professor Gilles Quispel, who urged the Jung Foundation in Zurich to purchase them as a birthday present for psychoanalyst Carl Gustav Jung. Today we know that the collection is incomplete: some of the codices have been irreparably and definitively lost, while others continue to wander around the world, waiting to be recovered.

as the Gospel of Thomas, the Gospel of the Egyptians, and the Gospel of Truth.Certain authorised researchers consider part of the texts found in the Nag Hammadi codices to be the official Gospels. Furthermore, some audacious investigators in search of truth beyond human convenience, believe that these documents possess an extreme and unique degree of veracity. There are various reasons for this belief: first of all, as these documents were written for an Egyptian public rather than a Roman one, they did not suffer from the misrepresentations displayed in texts translated for the latter. For this same reason, these manuscripts were exempt from Roman orthodox censorship. Last but not least, those who have studied them consider it highly possible that the texts are based on first-hand sources, such as accounts told by the collaborators of Jesus and by eye witnesses of the Jewish people's forced exodus from the Holy Land.

THE DEAD SEA SCROLLS

These were are a collection of approximately six hundred papyrus scrolls, written in Hebrew and Aramaic, that were discovered from 1947 onwards within a series of caves in present day Jordan, Northwest of the Dead Sea (in the region of Qirbet Qumran). This is why they are also known as the Qumran manuscripts. Attributed to a Jewish congregation living in the Qumran area at the time, the scrolls are thought to have formed part of the community's library. Carbon dating and textual analysis indicate that the majority of them were written between 200 BC and 68 AD. The papyrus scrolls include discipline manuals, Biblical commentaries, hymns, apocalyptic texts, two of the oldest copies found to date of the Book of Isaiah (practically intact) and multiple fragments from the Old Testament, from all of the books except the Book of Esther. Included in the Old Testament fragments is a wonderful paraphrase of the Book of Genesis. In addition, texts belonging to several of the apocryphal, deuterocanonical and pseudepigraphal books were also discovered among the scrolls, examples of which are: the Book of Tobias, the Ecclesiasticus, Jubilees and parts of the Book of Enoch. None of these texts were included within the canonical Bible. Researchers have found the numerous links between the ideas and idioms appearing in the Qumran manuscripts and those featuring in the New Testament text of particular interest: both of these texts stress the imminence of the Kingdom of Heaven, the necessity of immediate repentance and the hoped-for defeat of Evil. Furthermore, references to the baptism of the Holy spirit resemble each other and believers are portrayed in a similar way in the two sets of documents.

Most of the scroll collection was acquired partly by the Hebrew University of Jerusalem, and partly by the Syriac monastery of Saint Mark in Jerusalem. The Israeli government subsequently secured the latter part of the documents.

Fragment from the Book of Isaiah manuscript.

JESUS ACCORDING TO THE GNOSTICS

As mentioned above, the Nag Hammadi papyri and other Gnostic writings found had been produced for an Egyptian public, and were therefore exempt from Roman orthodox censorship. In addition, they were most probably based on first-hand sources. Consequently, it is not surprising that the Nag Hammadi manuscripts and other apocryphal Gospels contain passages contradicting orthodox writings and revealing to us aspects of Jesus, and of those around him, that we were unaware of. How is Jesus portrayed in these documents? In order to summarize, we could say the following: in comparison to the easily comprehensible Jesus – accessible to all – who emerges from the canonical Gospels, Gnostic writings reveal an esoteric Jesus, possessor of concealed knowledge that is reserved for only the initiated: the multiple secrets of the Heavens, the creation of man and the universe, the essence of Salvation, etc.

According to Gnosticism, Jesus took on the appearance of a man, descended into Hell and then arrived in this world in order to preach the exoteric part of his doctrine. These teachings were simple and easy to understand and were expressed through the use of parables. After appearing to die, Jesus ascended to Heaven and the Father, later on returning to this world to teach his disciples the esoteric and hidden side of his doctrine.

Jesus as presented in these texts is the living Lord; he is the resurrected Jesus who confided in his closest friends and revealed to them that which had never been heard by others before. According to Gnostic writings, Jesus was not a material or historical Christ, he was not a master, nor a teacher, nor the protagonist of miracles; he was the spiritual guide who revealed how the Kingdom of God was not something external, but an internal reality that everyone could potentially discover through knowledge of God and knowledge of oneself.

This is why Gnostic teachings encouraged direct communication with God, regardless of any ecclesiastical authority; this last point, of course, must have proved prejudicial to the Catholic Church (which, with the passing of time, would become an extremely powerful institution). According to the Gnostics, those who attained 'gnosis' or knowledge would become equal to the Deity. The Kingdom of the Father was a state of transformed or altered consciousness (similar to the Nirvana of Hindus or to the state of altered reality attained by shamans), where man would no longer be in need of a master or guide. According to this doctrine, whoever was able to experience an internal vision of Jesus would possess an equal or even superior authority to that of the apostles. Once again, let us think about the detrimental effect of this ideological position on the Church: it entailed a clear confrontation with the authority of priests and bishops, who viewed themselves as the successors to the apostle Peter. Moreover, Jesus as portrayed in Gnostics writings denied the idea that with him all prophecies would be fulfilled.

Some of the images of Christ presented in these Gospels may prove to be shocking. For example, within the miraculous Infancy Gospels, Jesus is portrayed as an extremely bright boy who is nevertheless eminently human and that, at times, proves to be undisciplined, prone to violence and scandalous demonstrations and who displays an often irresponsible exercise of his powers. Specifically, in one instance he beats another boy, who has offended him, to death.

In the Second Treatise of the Great Seth, Jesus is said to have eluded death on the cross through the use of an ingenious series of substitutions. The following fragment – where Jesus speaks in the first person – is a faithful copy of the book:

It was another, his father, who drank the bile and the vinegar; not I. I was beaten with a cane; it was another, Simon, who carried the cross on his shoulders. They placed the crown of thorns on another...and I was laughing at their ignorance.

Another shocking image is that of Christ confronting the Father with the following claim: 'give to me what is mine'. This was characteristic of some Gnostic theories that claimed parents should be hated and loved at the same time.

JESUS AND MARY MAGDALENE ACCORDING TO GNOSTIC SCRIPTURES

However, from all of the unknown facets of Jesus described in these books, we hold a particular interest in one: the relationship between Jesus and Mary Magdalene, the trust put in her and the esteem in which he held her, and, of course, the specific type of love he professed for her.

Let us now look at our first point: as described in the Gospel of Thomas, Jesus repeatedly praised Mary Magdalene in different ways and held her as a visionary, superior to any of the apostles. Furthermore, the Gospel of Mary describes her as being favoured with a series of visions and a perception highly superior to that of Peter; hence, we could infer that Magdalene was also an apostle, even though this has not been admitted or approved by orthodox believers.

In the Dialogue of the Saviour, Jesus refers to Magdalene as a 'woman who knows All'. In the Sophia of Jesus Christ, a non-protagonist Peter is portrayed as fiercely unable to accept the privileged position bestowed by Jesus onto Mary Magdalene. Jesus ignores his protests and reprimands him, but Magdalene confesses to him in private that she feels intimidated by Peter and that she is unable to speak freely in front of the apostle due to his hostility towards the female sex. In view of this, Christ comforts her and assures her that anybody inspired by the Spirit (regardless of their gender) could express their views on divine matters without fear.

Moving forward in our argument: in terms of carnal love, what were Jesus' feelings towards Mary Magdalene? Within multiple passages of

Mary Magdalene.

the Gnostic Gospels we find a repeated insistence on two facts: Magdalene was the companion of Jesus (later on we shall look at what this term implies), and she was the most loved among all of his disciples.

In the Gospel according to Philip, two very suggestive images are repeatedly emphasized: that of a bridal chamber and that of Magdalene as the 'companion' of Jesus. Let us look at each one of these in turn: regarding the bridal chamber image, the following text can be read: 'The Lord did everything in a mystery, a baptism and a chrism and a eucharist and a redemption and a bridal chamber.' Although at a first reading the concept of a bridal chamber may be understood as being of a metaphoric or symbolic character (as is often the case with expressions in religious texts), the fact is that numerous experts and scholars agree on interpreting the term literally.

The term 'companion' is a similar case; it is present, among other passages, in the following: 'there were three who always walked with the Lord; Mary, his mother, his sister and Magdalene, who was named his companion'. In this particular passage, from the multiple meanings that could be attributed to the word 'companion' (in what sense does she accompany Jesus? And until where does she accompany him?), scholars have determined that the term must be understood as meaning 'spouse' or 'wife', in the sense of a lasting bond between two people that involves – of course – sexual contact.

The Gospel according to Philip is even more explicit regarding this subject. We need only cite the following passage:

And the Saviour's companion was Mary Magdalene. But Christ loved her more than all of the other disciples and would often kiss her on the mouth. The rest of the disciples were offended by this and expressed disapproval.

Many of the apocryphal Gospel passages relate accounts of a bitter dispute without respite between Peter and Mary Magdalene, due to Peter's jealousy of the love Jesus professed for her. Specifically, in the Gospel of Mary, Peter purports to know Jesus loved Mary Magdalene over all other women and, hence, he angrily asks his disciples: 'Did he then speak in private with a woman and not openly with us? Are we all to turn around and listen to her? Did he prefer her to us?' Further on in the text, one of the disciples replies to Peter: 'Probably, as the Saviour knows her very well. This is why he loved her more than us.'

The Gospel of Mary also pronounces the following:

Peter told Mary: 'Sister, we are aware that the Saviour loved you more than he did all other women. Repeat to us all of the Saviour's words that you can remember – those that you know but we don't, as we haven't heard them before.' Mary answered the following: 'That which is hidden from you, I will proclaim to you.'

From all of the above apocryphal quotes we can clearly discern three major issues, which – by the way – were all conveniently silenced in the selection made by Christian orthodoxy when constituting the canonical Gospels. One of these issues is that Christ considered Mary Magdalene to be of a truly superior status; as previously quoted, Magdalene is a woman who knows 'All'. A second issue is the fully human and erotic nature of the feelings professed by Jesus to Magdalene. And a third matter (and most probably in consequence of the former two other matters) is the marriage bond that united them both: Mary Magdalene was known to all as the 'companion' of Jesus.

THE MARRIAGE OF CHRIST

Did Jesus Christ get married? In order to answer this question we must take a look at the official or canonical Gospels (rather than at the apocryphal ones), as they offer the observant reader a myriad of clues regarding the marriage of Christ. We must also study the norms and traditions held by the society of the time, and we can bring these to light through historical research (beyond what is related in the Bible).

It is true that there is no specific mention regarding Jesus' marital status in the official Gospels. In fact, we encounter a complete silence regarding this subject. But let us dwell upon some of the matters in question: the canonical Gospels state that many of Christ's disciples were married; in fact, nowhere in the text can we find Jesus defending celibacy. Furthermore, in the Gospel of Matthew, Jesus proclaims the following:

Have you not read that he who created them at the beginning, created them male and female? Consequently man will leave father and mother and unite himself to his wife and they will both become a single flesh.

If Jesus did not preach in favour of celibacy, what would be a valid reason to suppose that he practised what he did not preach? Jesus had many outstanding characteristics, one of them being – without a doubt – that he lived according to what he preached; there existed no gap, no contradiction between what he thought and said, and what he did.

Moreover, according to the Judaic custom of the time, celibacy was greatly frowned upon; it was believed that a man should get married – this was practically compulsory. Therefore, among a Jewish father's duties was that of finding a suitable wife for his son. To remain single was not a matter of 'choice' as it might be looked at nowadays; bachelorhood was perceived as a sort of stigma, constituting a serious deviation from the traditions and conventions held dear at the time. The belief in marriage was so strong that a Jewish author writing during the 1st century AD compared deliberate celibacy with murder. Let us remind ourselves at this point that, in the majority of cases, writers, just like all other artists, tend to give expression to the feelings and convictions of a community at a certain period in time. Therefore, if an author displayed such level of certitude regarding marriage, surely he was not the only one within his community who felt that way. Moreover, if remaining celibate was considered a stigma, something that would not have passed unnoticed, but that negatively marked an individual in a very public manner, how can we explain that there is not a single passage in the Bible referring to such an important 'detail'? If Jesus, as is stated by subsequent tradition, had remained celibate, it seems odd that none of the canonical Gospel passages refer to the fact. Therefore, it does not seem illogical to presume that the lack of allusion to this matter suggests that Jesus conformed to the norms and conventions of his era and was, consequently, married.

Charles Davis, a well respected modern scholar of theological matters, points at the fact that if Jesus had insisted on remaining a bachelor and, thus, in celibacy, his 'abnormal' behaviour would have been so scandalous that it would be impossible not to find traces within the Gospels of the reactions provoked by his stance.

Furthermore, in the Fourth Gospel we find an episode related to a marriage ceremony that could well have been that of Jesus: the transformation of water into wine at the marriage at Cana.

According to the text, this was a modest local ceremony, of a couple who remain anonymous. Jesus is 'called upon' to attend these nuptials, and (without an explanation) his mother is also present. For reasons not explained in the text either, Mary asked Jesus to replenish the wine – an act that would have normally been performed by either the homeowner or the bridegroom's family. Why then would Jesus be asked to do this, unless this was, in fact, his own wedding? We find more direct clues appearing immediately after the performance of the wine miracle, when 'the master of ceremonies called upon the bridegroom and told him: "everybody serves the good wine first and, when all are drunk, the inferior wine is served. But you have kept the good wine behind up until now."' These words are spoken to Jesus but, according to the Gospel text, they are spoken to the groom; thus, the implication is clear: the wedding is that of Jesus Christ himself. And, of course, if Christ married, his wife (in accordance to all that we have been expounding) could have been no other than Mary Magdalene. Hence, the question that ensues is: who was Mary Magdalene, wife of Jesus?

MARY MAGDALENE, WIFE OF JESUS

Mary of the town of Migdal or Magdala, in Galilee, was the beloved wife of Christ, and she is commonly portrayed as having been a repentant prostitute; however...was this really her profession? Beyond popular tradition, nowhere in the Gospels (neither apocryphal nor canonical) is it stated that Magdalene had been a prostitute. As can be appreciated by the reader, the Magdalene of Gnostic writing is described at all times as a woman of great wisdom and at no point in the text can we find allusions to her having been a prostitute; nor do they appear in the canonical Gospels either. If this is so, why has she been branded a prostitute by popular history? The reason for this seems to lie on the first occasion on which she is mentioned (in the Gospel of Luke), when she is referred to as a woman from whom had emerged seven demons. This image may be understood as a kind of exorcism performed on Magdalene by Jesus, which would then imply that she was 'possessed'; on the other hand, it could have been referring to some sort of conversion or initiation ritual linked to a goddess cult (Astarte or Ishtar, most probably) and consisting of seven stages. In the former instance, the idea of a 'possessed' Magdalene could in time have developed into that of a 'sinner' Magdalene, later on turning into the concept of her as a prostitute. Regarding our second interpretation of the demon image, if Magdalene were indeed part of a pagan cult, this would have certainly made her a prostitute in the eyes of those who divulged the Testaments, particularly after the Council of Nicaea took place.

Another possible reason for her being thought of as unchaste is the popular identification of Mary Magdalene with the penitent 'sinner woman' mentioned in the Gospel of Luke, who dried her tears from Jesus' feet with her hair and then anointed them. In the Gospel of John, the protagonist of this same scene was changed, stating that it was actually Mary, the sister of Jesus, who bathrf and anointed his feet. But it is mainly the term 'sinner' that seems to have rooted itself firmly in popular tradition regarding this woman. This might be explained by the fact that it was a 'hierodule' or 'consecrated priestess' who performed the sacred anointing of the 'sacrificial husband' in priestess-orientated cults, which could in its turn lead to the idea of a 'sacred prostitute' anointing the feet of Jesus. Furthermore, anointment used to form part of marriage ceremonies in ancient times, symbolizing the union between the groom and his royal bride's people and land.

In reality, Mary Magdalene was a descendant of the tribe of Benjamin, just as Christ descended from the tribe of David. This means they both descended from royalty – royal blood ran in their veins. When their houses were united by marriage and their two bloodlines linked, the result was a political (as well as a loving) union, legitimately entitled to claim the throne and restore their royal lineage to power. The reason why the Church would later on decide to conceal – among many other facts – Mary Magdalene's true origins thus becomes clear: Magdalene's royal ancestry constituted an infallible threat to the ever-growing power of Christian orthodoxy. Moreover, Mary Magdalene and her marriage to Jesus are highly connected to two other concepts permeating good part of *The Da Vinci Code*: the goddess cult and sacred matrimony, or sex.

THE GODDESS: THE PRINCIPLE OF DIVINE FEMININITY

We now turn to the apocryphal Gospels once more, as they have the power to shed light over that which has been hidden or silenced by the Church.

A fragment from the Nag Hammadi manuscripts known by the title of 'The Thunder, Perfect Mind' speaks about a goddess, a female power who reveals the following:

For I am the first and the last.
I am the honoured one and the scorned one.
I am the whore and the saint.
I am the wife and the virgin.
I am the mother and the daughter...
I am that one whose wedding is grand and has taken no husband.
I am knowledge and ignorance.
I am strength and fear.
I am stupid and wise.
I have no God, and I am one whose God is great.

In the Secret Book of James, it is revealed that the Mother, also known as Barbelo, was the female principle of the Father, while he was her counterweight, her complementary other.

In the Gospels of Philip and Thomas, we encounter the image of the Divine Mother, Sophia, the personification of Wisdom, the original creator of the universe from whom all living creatures were born.

In the the Hypostasis of the Archons, God encounters an extremely powerful female deity, and the following dialogue ensues between them:

...and he turned around arrogantly, proclaiming: 'It is I who is God, and there is no other apart from me...' A voice arose above the kingdom of absolute power, and it announced: 'You are mistaken, Samael (God of the blind).' And he replied: 'If something other existed before I, let it reveal itself.' And immediately Sophia extended a finger and brought light into matter, and followed it into the region of Chaos... And he told his offspring once more: 'It is I who is the God of Everything.' And Life, the daughter of Wisdom, cried out, and said to him: 'You are mistaken, Saklas!'

According to the Gnostic Ptolemy in his *Letter to Flora*, Sophia is the intermediary between the soul of the material world (the demiurge) and the world of ideas or plenitude (the pleroma). The pleroma forms an

Phoenician goddess Astarte.

essential part of primordial man; however, it abandoned him, and so man cannot attain salvation without finding it again.

The notion of the female linked to the divine appearing in Gnostic texts carries certain implications, but what are they? Primitive Christianity believed in the concept of sacred femininity, but the Church would later on omit this archetype from its creed. As explained in *The Da Vinci Code*, no one has put more effort into effacing the history of the goddess than the Catholic Church.

What is the history of goddess worship, of the cult of the goddess? Let us look into it: in all prehistoric cultures (as well as in many later ones), the central cosmogonic figure, the power or creative force behind the formation of the universe, was personified by the female form; her generative and protective powers were portrayed by highly pronounced female attributes: buttocks, breasts, pregnant belly and vulva. This goddess, divine uterus from which everything is born, and to which everything returns in order to regenerate and maintain the cycle of nature, was named the Great Goddess or Great Mother; the Great Goddess presided over humanity's religious expression in an exclusive manner from, approximately, 30,000 BC.

Those early societies were governed by female principle, regarding the earth as mother, and death and inhumation as a return to her belly. These pre-agricultural and primitive agricultural cultures developed a type of cosmic religion that involved the constant and periodic renovation of life, and whose object of cult was the Mother Goddess. According to this concept, the earth was the mother of everything; plants, animals and human beings were all considered to be her children, and were thus tied to her rule and designs. The high status of the Mother Goddess is reflected as far back as the Palaeolithic in the famous Venus of Willendorf, a limestone sculpture dating back to about 26,000 BC. Other extant sculptures are even more ancient – although less well known – such as a series of female-form statuettes dating back to around 30,000 BC. These small figures measure between 3 to 22 cms in height; sculpted out of stone, bone, and ivory, they represent women, emphasizing in particular the maternal aspects of the female shape. The figurines' vulvas, breasts, buttocks and pregnant bellies are enhanced, in sharp contrast to the representation of their heads and extremities, which appear far less defined.

Within these Mother Goddess mythologies, the following constitute fundamental motifs: the mystery of female sexuality, the enigma of conception and birth, the link between the female cycle and the lunar cycle and the idea of the earth as maternal belly. This Primeval Goddess was unique and embodied in her form all life forces: birth, life, death and rebirth. All women were her priestesses and, therefore, servants to her will, while they were also earthly representatives of her power.

However, as we pointed out above, the importance of the goddess was not a prerogative of prehistoric times; in different ways, and holding different attributes, the goddess also appears in various other cultures.

For the Egyptians, the goddess Isis holds both divine and human powers and is the inventor of agriculture. In ancient Mesopotamia, we find the goddess Ninlil, who was revered for teaching people how to cultivate the earth. In ancient Sumerian culture, the goddess Nidaba was hailed as the inventor of clay tablets and the art of writing. Within Hindu mythology, the female deity Sarasvati is believed to have invented the alphabet. In Greece and in Çatal Hüyük, grain offerings were performed within the sanctuaries of goddesses. We could also mention Ishtar (in Babylon), Freya (in Scandinavia), Anat (in Canaan) and Astarte (in Phoenicia), among numerous other female deities who reigned during ancient times.

However, what is truly important is not the concept of a female deity as such, but the understanding of the world and human beings (as well as their relationships) that this entails. As Mother Goddess, she possesses the former's characteristics: she is the one who bestows life, who protects who loves all of her children equally and unconditionally.

With the passing of time, and through various circumstances, this type of matriarchal culture, where the female principle is fundamental, gradually disappeared. Through a cumulative process of transformation, the male god took its place, dispossessing women of their ancestral power, while depositing it instead in the hands of men and of a male deity who would represent them. The process of creation ceased to be understood through a simile involving female reproductive physiology, and went on to be portrayed as the end result of male power instruments.

Once again, when looking at the transition from the female deity to the male, what really matters is that we understand the concept lying behind this change. The omnipotent (and even authoritarian) male god is strikingly different from the female goddess, who is a nurturing mother who loves her children unconditionally. The male god can in some ways be terrifying; he punishes his children and gives preference to some over others. Consequently, with the emergence and later empowerment of the almighty male deity, appeared a clergy with a clearly pyramidal power structure, together with a class-divided society and the institution of monarchy. Meanwhile, the power held by the goddess gradually decreased, as did that of mortal women.

SACRED SEX AND MATRIMONY: WOMAN AND MAN ARE BOTH TWO AND THE SAME

The concept of a couple's sexual union holding a sacramental function is a highly alien one to contemporary Western culture. Nevertheless, a large number of prior civilisations tried to understand the universe, and to gain access to higher levels of knowledge, by dissolving the self in order to unite time and eternity. In doing this, their aim was to develop supernatural capabilities, approaching divinity and immortality in the process. Although to modern Western culture the term 'holy sex' involves a sort of contradiction, we are about to look at a striking fact. Practically all of antiquity's religious systems – including those of Egypt, India and China – developed sacramental and magical sex rituals, a tradition that persists to date in – for example – practices such as that of Tantric sex.

Jesus and Mary Magdalene embody the 'holy spouses' archetype existing in Middle Eastern goddess cults, as well as in many other ancestral cultures: Shiva and Shakty in Hindu culture, or the Sumerian couple

SACRED SEX AMONG THE GNOSTICS

Some Gnostic groups saw in the sexual act an image of the much wanted union with divinity, and they basically achieved this symbolic image through the bridal chamber ceremony. In this ceremony a bedroom was prepared, and within it a man and a woman celebrated their physical union – which did not reach full carnal fusion – while performing prayers and anointments: all of this represented the definitive union with the heavenly deity. However, other Gnostics went even further and performed ritualistic orgies: a meal abundant in meat and wine was prepared, and after it the ceremony of 'agape' or love would begin. During this ceremony, men and women would join in indiscriminate manner, while semen – symbolizing the body of Christ – and menstrual blood – symbolizing the blood of Christ – were served as an offering.

formed by Inanna and her lover, the divine Dumuzi. Regarding the latter couple, a remaining ancient Sumerian text (of incalculable value) allows an insight into the sensual nature of the 'hieros gamos' or holy matrimony ritual:

And so Inanna says: 'My vulva, the horn, the boat to Paradise, is full of longing like the new moon. My unploughed land lays ready for sowing. Regarding me, Innana: who will plough my land? Who will plough my high fields? Who will plough my damp land?'
Dumuzi replies to her: 'Great Lady, the king will plough your vulva. I, Dumuzi, will plough your vulva.'
And to this Innana, Queen of Paradise, impatiently retorts: 'Then plough my vulva, man of my heart! Plough my vulva!'

Just like the goddess, the concept of holy matrimony and its sexual counterpart are ancient. We can also find their presence in Gnostic texts, which speak of God (that is both Father and Mother) in terms of a sacred and divine couple, a unification of the male and female deities. In the Gospel of Thomas we may read: 'when you manage to achieve that man is not man anymore, and woman is not woman': a clear allusion to the merging of the eternal masculine with the eternal feminine.

THE CHILDREN OF JESUS?

If Jesus did not remain celibate and married Mary Magdalene, did they have descendants? Not only is it probable, it is practically absurd to surmise the contrary. As they were married, the fact of children cannot – in practical and logical terms – be questioned; it cannot be doubted. So what happened to Christ's wife after he was crucified? Some of Jesus' disciples (including Joseph of Arimathea) smuggled the pregnant Mary Magdalene from Jerusalem to Alexandria, from where she was taken to southern France (named Gaul in those times). In this way, Mary Magdalene carried the 'Holy Grail' – the 'San Greal' in French, which can also be read as 'Sang Real', literally translating as 'Royal Blood' – to the Gallic coast, arriving in a boat without oars, fleeing from Palestine. Mary Magdalene tried to adapt to her new homeland as smoothly as possible. It was hard for her at the beginning, but with time and kind support and refuge from Gaul's Jewish community, she managed. She subsequently had a daughter, Sarah, who was brought up in France. To summarize, Jesus sowed his seed in the body of Mary Magdalene; the pregnant Mary then became the 'Holy Grail', the bearer of her crucified husband's royal blood.

(from left to right) Catholic imagery announces that Jesus Christ King will return to this world in order to implant the social kingdom of His Sacred Heart. King Clovis I, the first Merovingian monarch. The four sons of King Clovis I, among which the Frankish kingdom was distributed. King Dagobert II, the last Merovingian monarch, who was murdered.

And so it was Sarah who continued the royal lineage of Jesus. This royal bloodline later on became the Merovingian dynasty, the first of the Frankish kings.

Not surprisingly, the Merovingians were monarchs linked to numerous mysteries. Although the Merovingian monarchy's customs seem not to have differed greatly from other customs of its period, the fact is that this was a dynasty of kings constantly enveloped in an aura of mystery, legend, magic and – what would nowadays be termed – supernatural phenomena, even when they were alive. According to tradition, they were well versed in the esoteric sciences; they were also initiated in the arcane arts and were followers of occultism. The Merovingians were often named the 'sorcerer kings' or 'miracle-working monarchs'. Interestingly enough, many of the chronicles of the period referred to their special healing powers, which were believed to hold their origins in the miraculous properties of their blood. For example, it was believed at the time that the Merovingian kings were capable of curing illnesses simply by placing their hands on someone, or by using the tassels adorning the hems of their garments. Consequently, the question arises: why did people talk about miracle cures when referring to this dynasty? And above all, why were their exceptional healing powers assigned to their blood, when they could have been attributed to any other cause? Why was Merovingian royal blood thought of as being of a miraculous, divine and sacred nature? The only plausible answer is that they had inherited this miraculous capability from their distant ancestor: Christ himself. Furthermore, it was also understood at the time that all Merovingian monarchs had carried a birthmark over their heart that set them apart from the rest of men and served as a testimony to their partly divine blood: we once more encounter the concept of divine blood and divine ancestry.

In addition, the Merovingian dynasty's attitude towards Judaism seems to stand unparalleled in Western history prior to the Lutheran reformation. Disregarding the Church of Rome's continuing protests, they were tolerant and understanding of the Jewish community: mixed marriages were frequent and numerous Jews occupied high-ranking posts. Additionally, the Merovingian royal family and the families related to it, had a surprising number of Jewish names: one of the brothers of King Clotaire II was given the name Samson, a Count of Rosellón was named Solomon, and there was an abbot named Elisachar, which is a variation of Lazarus.

But, what happened to the Merovingian dynasty?

In 496 AD, the Church made a pact agreeing to remain perpetually committed to the Merovingian royal bloodline. It is likely that in doing this, the Church was well aware of the true identity of the royal lineage. During these 'committed' times, King Clovis I was offered the prestigious rank of Sacred Roman Emperor by the Church. Later on however, the Church betrayed the Merovingians, and took part in the murder of King Dagobert II. It is obvious than in doing this, their objective was to completely eradicate the Merovingian royal bloodline. The true descendants of – a mostly human – Jesus were starting to become a source of problems and conflict for the orthodox Church, which was based on a centralized power that heralded as its theoretical and philosophical basis the divinity of Jesus (see: Constantine and the Council of Nicaea). Nevertheless, despite all of the efforts put into making the Merovingians disappear from the face of the earth, the royal stock survived: mainly through King Dagobert's son, Sigebert III, whose descendants managed to save themselves from persecution. During the following centuries, the Merovingian dynasty – aided by the Priory of Sion – made repeated efforts to recuperate their lost heritage (see: The Merovingians and the restitution of power). On various occasions they were extremely close to success, but they were stopped before achieving it by different causes: adverse circumstances, errors of judgement and imponderable events. Most importantly though, and beyond these temporary drawbacks, the lineage has not been extinguished and the descendants of Christ are still among us. As the reader will be able to appreciate further on in this book, the Merovingian dynasty does not only still exist today, but it is also willing to return to power, aided in its endeavour by the *Prieuré de Sion*.

CONSTANTINE AND THE COUNCIL OF NICAEA

As we are all aware, not of the human aspects of Jesus – who was a husband and a father – nor the divine status of the goddess and the feminine, nor the individual's non-prescribed experience of divinity are to be found in

THE MEROVINGIAN DYNASTY AND ITS RESTITUTION TO POWER

Once it had been removed from power, the Merovingian House made repeated attempts to redeem its former status. These attempts were performed by means of three essentially different, yet complementary, strategies. One of their strategies involved creating a sort of psychological climate, the objective of which was to erode the spiritual hegemony of Rome. This strategic current gained expression in Hermetic thought and in occult writings. A second programme aimed at the reclaiming of their birthright through political intrigue and machinations. And a third plan was designed to retrieve their heritage through dynastic marriages. A possible (and logical) question ensues: would it not have been easier to reveal and prove their origins instead, so as to gain immediate world recognition? If they had done this though, things would not have been as simple as they might at first seem. A 'premature' revelation of this stature would – most probably – have triggered a bitter war between different political factions, and the Merovingian dynasty would have experienced great difficulty in resisting this struggle unless it was already placed in a position of authority. Therefore, it was necessary to restore their sovereignty first and, only then, reveal the truth about their ancestry. To date they have not managed it...yet.

orthodox Christianity or in the 'official' Gospels. This lamentable situation remains in place to date, and a specific year can be traced back as its starting point: 325 AD, the year in which the Council of Nicaea took place.

Gnostic Christianity, as we saw earlier, is based upon personal experience and the believer's personal union with the divine. This freethinking ideology undermined the authority of bishops and priests and so it became necessary to encourage a blind faith in the single dogma of the Church, in a doctrine that dismissed all individual speculation.

The Church needed a fixed structure of principles that had to be clearly codified and have absolutely no fissures that could allow free individual interpretation.

Emperor Constantine the Great did a lotto promote this. First of all he called together the Council of Nicaea and, later on, he supported orthodox Christianity through various actions.

Constantine was, in fact, a pagan emperor who was baptized and converted to Christianity only on his deathbed. Throughout his entire life he held the post of high priest to the sun worship cult – the 'Sol Invictus' or 'Invincible Sun' cult – a religion of Assyrian origin that Roman emperors had imposed on all of their subjects.

However, despite his pagan beliefs, Constantine could clearly see that, three centuries after the Crucifixion had taken place, religious tendencies among his subjects were becoming increasingly accentuated. Christians and pagans had begun to quarrel, something that posed a serious threat to the cohesion of the Roman Empire. The emperor's objective then became the territorial, political, *and* religious unity of his territories. This is why he summoned the Council of Nicaea, in order to unify the Roman Empire under a sole religion: Christianity. Christian orthodoxy had numerous points in common with the Sol Invictus cult, and so this made it possible for Constantine to combine and standardize both religious beliefs into a single doctrine.

Effigy of Constantine, the first monotheistic Roman emperor.

The Council of Nicaea was the first ecumenical assembly to ever take place, and was gathered by the emperor Constantine, with the approval of Pope Sylvester I. In excess of three hundred priests attended the gathering and the Pope sent a Legate as his representative. Among other resolutions, the council issued several regulations defining the authority of bishops. It was also decided by popular vote that Jesus was God, and not a human prophet. As a basis to all of this, the council passed the so-called Nicaean Creed:

We believe in one God, the Father, the Almighty,
maker of heaven and earth,
of all that is, seen and unseen.
We believe in one Lord, Jesus Christ,
the only Son of God,
eternally begotten of the Father,
God from God, light from light,

true God from true God,
begotten, not created, of one Being with the Father;
through him all things were made.
For us and for our salvation he came down from heaven,
by the power of the Holy Spirit he was born of the Virgin Mary,
and became truly human.
For our sake he was crucified under Pontius Pilate;
he suffered death and was buried.
On the third day he rose again in accordance with the Scriptures;
he ascended into heaven and is seated at the right hand of the Father.
He will come again in glory to judge the living and the dead,
and his kingdom will have no end.
We believe in the Holy Spirit, the Lord, the giver of life,
who proceeds from the Father [and the Son],
who with the Father and the Son is worshipped and glorified,
who has spoken through the prophets.
We believe in one holy catholic and apostolic Church.
We acknowledge one baptism for the forgiveness of sins.
We look for the resurrection of the dead,
and the life of the world to come. Amen.

With the sanctioning of this creed, Jesus went from being regarded as a mortal prophet to being hailed as the Son of God, and it must be obvious to the reader that this was no minor happening. To establish that Christ's nature was of a divine origin was of fundamental importance to the further unification of the Roman Empire that followed. It was also essential to the imposition of the ideology on which the Vatican's power was based: in proclaiming him the Son of God, Constantine made Jesus into an unquestionable entity whose power reached far beyond the human world. In this way, he smothered any possible pagan threat to Christianity, while at the same time leaving the followers of Jesus with only one way to redemption: the Roman Catholic Apostolic Church.

Later on, Constantine himself sanctioned the confiscation and destruction of all texts questioning the orthodox teachings of the Church, including works by Christians considered to be 'heretics', as well as works by pagan authors containing any reference whatsoever to Jesus. Another extremely important event was when Constantine imposed the assignment of a fixed income to the Catholic Church. Last but not least, in 331 AD, he commissioned and financed the writing of new copies of the Bible. These were constructed, obviously, in accordance to the official version of the Church, and were carefully supervized by the custodians of Christian orthodoxy.

CHAPTER 2

THE PRIORY OF
SION, THE
KNIGHTS
TEMPLAR AND
THE HOLY GRAIL

THE PRIORY OF SION, THE KNIGHTS TEMPLAR AND THE HOLY GRAIL

The Priory of Sion and the Knights Templar constituted – to use a metaphor – the two sides of a single coin. The Priory was the hidden side of the coin: secret, arcane, and clandestine. The Knights Templar, however, were exposed to the world, and acted as the military front of the Priory. Nevertheless, both organizations held a similar purpose or goal: to recover (the Knights Templar) and to guard (the Priory of Sion) a set of secret documents revealing the true essence of the Holy Grail. These documents demonstrate the actual role of Mary Magdalene as wife of Jesus Christ and carrier of their royal lineage. With the marriage of Jesus and Magdalene, the royal houses of David and Benjamin were united, and their ancestral royal bloodline – stemming from the monarchy existing in times of King Solomon – was continued through the birth of their daughter Sarah. According to the manuscripts protected by the Priory, Sarah was born in France and has descendants even to this date. Additionally, the Priory's publicly confessed aim is to return the Merovingian kings to the throne.

But let us begin by relating the history of the visible front of the Priory of Sion: the Knights Templar. Afterwards, we will explore the essence of the Priory's secret nature. Lastly, we will narrate the fascinating and highly controversial story of that which links the two organizations: the Holy Grail.

A Templar knight.

THE KNIGHTS TEMPLAR

As mentioned above, The Knights Templar worked as the military counterpart and armed support forces of the Priory of Sion. The Templars constituted the archetype of the much-admired Crusader knight; forming part of the storm troops that conquered the Holy Land, they fought and died in the name of Jesus Christ. They personified that mythical figure of the medieval knight errant; fanatical warrior monks, they presented a memorable and striking image dressed in a white robe embroidered with a red cross (the famous Templar Cross).

The the Knights Templar lasted for approximately two hundred years, and they have been the source of numerous investigations since then. On the one hand, the Templars were Crusaders. On the other hand, and as it is explained in *The Da Vinci Code*, they were employed as the military arm of the Priory of Sion. However, they have also been accused of negating and repudiating both Jesus Christ and the Cross, and of being greedy, despotic and arrogant thugs. Numerous scholars and writers portray them as the servants of Satan; others believe them to be mystic initiates, guardians to mysterious knowledge and secret information that transcend Christian understanding and beliefs. In contrast, most recent historical studies tend to view them as the innocent and unfortunate victims of the power politics of the Church. But...who in actuality were the Knights Templar? In order to answer this question let us now turn to the two existing versions of their story. These versions are not contradictory, but complementary: the official history of the Knights Templar, and their second and more mysterious secret history.

THE OFFICIAL HISTORY OF THE KNIGHTS TEMPLAR

The Order of the Poor Knights of Christ and the Temple of Solomon was the real and complete name of the Knights Templar. It is generally presumed that a nobleman from the Champagne region, Hughes de Payen, founded the Order in 1118. At around that time, the Crusaders had managed to hold their post in Palestine and conquer Jerusalem, so a large number of pilgrims from Western Europe were making their way onto the Holy Land. A military order (the Knights Hospitalers) had been formed to distribute food and medicine among the poor and sick of Jerusalem. Nevertheless, the journey to the Holy Land continued to be a dangerous one where pilgrims remained exposed, among other difficulties, to highwaymen and bandits. Due to this state of affairs, the founder of the Templar order, together with eight of his comrades, made a proposal to

Baldwin I, Latin King of Jerusalem: Hughes de Payen and his fellow knights offered to ensure the safety of paths and roads leading to the Holy Land, as well as to guard over travelling pilgrims. The King of Jerusalem gladly accepted their offer. Once in Jerusalem, and in spite of having sworn an oath to live in poverty, the knights put themselves up in luxurious lodgings: the mansion they chose as their abode had, according to tradition, been built on top of the foundations of the ancient temple of Solomon; hence, the reason behind the name of the Order of the Temple. It seems that within approximately ten years, the knights' fame spread across most of Europe due – in great part – to the eulogies bestowed upon them by ecclesiastical authorities, who greatly praised their Christian endeavours. Around that same period of time, most of the Knights Templar (they were only nine in total) returned to Europe, and were greeted as triumphant heroes. Later on at the Council of Troyes, they were officially recognized and established as a religious and military order. The founder of the Order, Hughes de Payen, received the title of Grand Master. Both he and his subordinate knights would have to become warrior monks, and act according to very strict rules based on the Cistercian monastic order. These exacting rules included regulations on clothing, diet and numerous other aspects of the daily lives of these mystical soldiers. Once admitted to the Order, its members were held to an oath of poverty, chastity and obedience. They were forbidden to keep any possessions, and were not allowed to do anything without the permission of their superiors; every single action they took, every major or minor aspect of their new life as Templar knights – however insignificant it might have seemed – was severely regulated. The Templar Order rejected anything that it considered to be superfluous or mundane, and its knights could hold no property except for their personal items, three horses and a squire or servant. Due to their sworn vows, knights were also forbidden to embellish their clothing with any kind of frivolous ornamentation. They were not allowed to keep locked the arks and chests where they stored their personal belongings. In addition, they were not permitted to write or receive any letters without the relevant authorization. The knights were banned from travelling or changing their location (not even to attend religious ceremonies) without prior authorization from their superiors at their current residence. They were also forced to cut their hair, but were forbidden from doing the same to their beards (so making them easy to recognize), and they had to dress in the habit of the Order: a white cloak adorned with a red cross. According to the Templar norms of conduct, futile conversation, laughter, and jokes were all prohibited. Among themselves, as well as among other people outside the Order, they were expected to behave with humility and courtesy, and to

THE HIERARCHICAL ORDER OF THE KNIGHTS TEMPLAR

The Templar Order was divided into several different categories. These divisions were strictly regulated, and were held to their own specific rights, obligations and functions. What follows are the ranks of the Templar ladder:

- **Grand Master**: he was labelled the 'Prince of Christendom', and commonly resided in Jerusalem.
- **Seneschal**: acted as both a deputy and an adviser to the Grand Master. Because in theory (and often also in practice) he acted on behalf of the Grand Master, he enjoyed a similar status to him, and displayed the same emblems when on military campaigns.
- **Marshal**: he was in charge of the Order's martial activities.
- **Treasurer**: he was in charge of the financial and economic affairs of the Order.
- **Knight Commander**: he assisted the Treasurer. He was also responsible for the protection of travellers and pilgrims, which included aiding them and providing them with food, horses and suits of armour.
- **Knight Brothers**: they were also called just 'brothers'. The knight brothers all originated from aristocratic families (including the upper and the lower nobility). They performed the most high-end military functions, and were equipped as heavy cavalry.
- **Chaplains**: they were ordained priests and saw to the spiritual needs of the Order. The chaplains were dressed in black and were subject to the same obligations and rights as the knight brothers.
- **Sergeant Brothers**: these warriors were support troops and were equipped as light cavalry. The sergeant brothers were generally employed as aides or squires to the knight brothers and were drawn from a lower social class than them.
- **Drapier**: he was in charge of the members' garments, and also performed administrative duties.
- **Farmers, artisans, apothecaries, bakers**, etc: these workers preferred to be subject to the Templar Order than to a feudal lordship.

follow a dignified and refined code of conduct. If they were taken prisoner, they were not allowed to beg for mercy, and they had to fight to the death; they could only abandon a battle if they were outnumbered three to one. Moreover, because of their vow of poverty, if they they could not be ransomed, so they were often executed. When they died, they were wrapped in their cloak and lain face-down on a board and buried, without a name or marking of any kind, within a communal grave.

In principle, the Order of the Temple was directly responsible only to the Pope and, within the organization itself, to the Grand Master. Within a short time, the Templars widened their mission, and became responsible for actively pursuing the battle against Islam.

In 1139, Pope Innocent II passed a Papal bull declaring the Knights Templar an autonomous army, independent of kings, prelates and princes; they were now also free from political or religious interference. In this way, the Templars were transformed into an independent international empire. The Order's numbers increased in an exponentially during the twenty or so years that followed this Papal council. The sons of noble families eagerly enrolled, and donations in aid of the Templar mission (including land holdings and estates) arrived from all over. Lastly, in order to be admitted a man had to transfer all of his wealth to the Templar Order.

So, despite the Templar vow of poverty, the Order's treasury expanded to huge sums of money within a few decades. By 1160, the Order of the Poor Knights of Christ could not be described as poor any longer and held properties in Spain, Portugal, France, England, Scotland, Flanders, Germany, Austria, Hungary, Italy, and the Holy Land.

A Templar knight.

Over the following century, the Knights Templar gained international power, while their political activities crossed the borders of the Christian world: they established links with the Muslim world, including the Ismaelite assassin sect – the Islamic equivalent of the Templar Order. The Order's interests went far beyond the political, martial and diplomatic: they were the inventors of modern banking, and became the leading money

Baphomet, the mysterious demonic idol of the Knights Templar.

handlers of Europe, as well as providing their banking services to several wealthy Muslim magnates. This position arose partly because they had so much property that is was safer for kings and nobles away from home to trust their assets and precious goods to the custody of Templar castles and fortresses.

Their influence on other spheres was also highly important: they contributed to the development of surveying, cartography, navigation and road construction. In addition, the Order possessed its own shipyards and military and commercial fleets. It also had its own hospitals, which were equipped with state-of-the-art technology for their time, with doctors who understood and implemented modern principles of cleanliness and hygiene.

Aided by its wealth and varied activities, the Templar Order became increasingly affluent and powerful. As is commonly the case, this situation also resulted in its transformation into a more brutal, arrogant and corrupt organization. The European upper classes became jealous of the Order's grandeur and independence from the law, while the lower classes blamed it for oppressive taxes.

In the meantime, Christian forces were being virtually annihilated in the Holy Land and, by 1291, most of the territory had been re-conquered by Muslim forces. The Knights Templar continued to fight, while putting into practice innovative military strategies. However, with the final loss of the Holy Land to the Muslim world, the Templars' *raison d'être* was extinguished, and so they turned their attention to Europe.

By virtue of their regular contact with the Judaic and Islamic worlds, the Templars had absorbed numerous ideas, concepts and practices that were foreign to the orthodox Christianity of Rome, and that were not approved of by it in the least. For example, it was not completely unusual for the Order to employ Arab secretaries, or for the knights themselves to be fluent in that language.

Towards the beginning of the 14th century, Pope Clement V and Philip IV, King of France (where the Order was firmly established), started to wish that the Knights Templar would disappear from the face of the earth. The Pope considered them to be too dangerous, while King Philip wanted to banish the arrogant and powerful Templar knights from his lands; he had three major reasons: he was full of resentment towards the Order as he had applied for admission and had been rejected; he lusted after their immense wealth; and lastly, he was aware that they had become an independent state, practically parallel to his own in influence and strength, and this made him feel extremely threatened and anxious.

According to some versions it was the Pope, and according to others it was King Philip, who produced a list of accusations against the Templar knights. The list was based on accounts from spies who had infiltrated the Order, and on the confession of the odd recusant Templar knight. Secret arrest warrants containing the list of imputations were issued and delivered, together with the imposition that the letters be opened on 13 October 1307. At dawn that day, the sealed documents were opened and a list of varied accusations against the Templars was read; these included: heresy, desecration of the Cross, following a demonic cult, sodomy and a series of further blasphemous acts. Most of the Order's members were arrested, and many of them were burned at the stake as heretics.

BAPHOMET, THE MYSTERIOUS DEMONIC IDOL OF THE KNIGHTS TEMPLAR

When they were subjected to questioning following their arrest, several Templar knights made references to something named 'Baphomet', using a type of reverence towards it that bordered idolatry. Beyond the fact that in all of the knights' accounts the idea of this idol was associated with a head, it was never discovered what it was exactly. Depending on the confession in question, 'Baphomet' was alluded to in a varying manner, and was said to be all of the following:

• A dried and stuffed human head, which was black and demonic, and originated from Egypt.
• A woman's head made out of gilded silver that contained inside it two cranial bones; these were wrapped first in a white linen cloth, and then in a red one.
• A skull.
• A fetish made out of three human heads that were anointed with fat from the bodies of sacrificed children.

Nevertheless, one of the main objectives of the Pope and King Philip in taking this course of action was not accomplished. Neither the Pope nor the French monarch managed to secure the Order's fabulous wealth, and it is a fact that the wonderful Templar treasure remains hidden to this day. The Templars arrested in France were tried, tortured, and accused of several charges linked to heresy; these charges were the following:

Arrest of several Templar knights.

• Denying Christ by secretly forswearing his name, and holding secret meeting in which they worshipped some sort of idol named 'Baphomet' (see: 'Baphomet, the mysterious demonic idol of the Knights Templar').

• Following the blasphemous Marcion, who had publicly stated: 'Christ has nothing to do with Jehovah. The Old Testament is amoral. Christ is the son of an unknown God of Love, and all of the prophets – including John the Baptist – are servants to Jehovah, the false god.'

• Holding a secret admission process, in which the aspiring candidate was was expected to deny Christ and spit, tread and even urinate on the Christian Cross.

• Having allowed strange, and even heretical, doctrines to enter the Order, including Sufism, Islam, etc.

• Performing rituals which included sodomy and kissing the Grand Masters on their private parts.

• Threatening to kill anybody who revealed the Order's secret initiation rituals.

• Teaching women how to have an abortion.

• Committing infanticide.

In 1312, the Pope officially dissolved the Templar Order. In France however, they continued to be persecuted. Finally, in March 1314, Jacques de Molay, the Order's Grand Master, and Geoffroi de Charnay, the Seneschal of Normandy, were burned at the stake. With their execution, the Knights Templar disappeared from the grand stage of history; yet the truth is that they never ceased to exist. This was due partly to the large number of Templar members who managed to flee, and partly to the help and support that they received from numerous local leaders.

THE KNIGHTS' ADMISSION PROCESS

To be permitted to join the Order as members, applicants had to pass several entrance tests and rites, which entailed considerable difficulty and hardship. To begin with, they were assigned the least agreeable domestic tasks, such as cleaning, working in the vegetable plot or in the workshops, feeding and taking care of the animals, etc. They had to perform these lowly tasks with the servants, and should look contented when doing them.

When this first trial period was over, the future Knight Templar had to go through several further purification phases, which were as severe as they were difficult. These trial phases could last anything from two weeks to several months. If the applicant knight was able to pass them, he went on to the final phase of the admission process: this was a spiritual test, where he was confined in a small and dark room (eventually a prison cell or a cave) for the duration of a whole night. Within this dark room, an altar with a crucifix had been installed, and the aspiring candidate was expected to pass the entire night kneeling on the floor and praying in front of the altar. The reason behind this final test was that the candidate would identify with the Passion of Christ, and would then ask God for sufficient strength to accomplish his vows (that is, if he were to be admitted to the Order).

The Templar admission rite was supposedly inspired by ancient pre-Christian mysteries. It was magnificent, yet solemn and sober, and would inspire in the entrant an unforgettable feeling of spiritual elevation. At this ceremony, the entrant would have to relinquish all worldly interests and aspirations. Once he had been cross-examined, and had attentively listened to the Templar code of conduct and regulations, he would go on to the admission ceremony proper. This was performed at night, and all participating members had to meet at the Church of the Order. Halfway through the ceremony, the candidate was taken to the chapter house), where he would kneel in front of the Grand Master and ask to be admitted to the Order. The Grand Master would then put the novice through extensive questioning concerning his life up until that moment: was he married or had he been married in the past, did he have a girlfriend or lover, was he in good health, had he ever formed part of any other order, did he have any pending debts that he or his family could not pay back, was he or had he ever been a member of the clergy, had he ever been excommunicated, had he bribed a member of the Order so as to facilitate his admission to it, etc. If the novice's answers were satisfactory, the Grand Master would then ask him to recite his vows, which consisted in promising to God and to the Virgin Mary the following:

- Absolute obedience to the Grand Master and to his superiors (the novice's).
- Constant commitment and loyalty to the Order.
- Chastity.
- Lack of possessions.
- Total respect for the conduct regulations and traditions of the Order.
- To help in the conquest of the Holy Land of Jerusalem.

Once he had sworn to the above vows, the new Templar was finally admitted with the following promise: 'bread and water, meagre clothing and many penurious toils.' After this, he was dressed with the mantle of the Order and was handed the crucifix and sword. The Grand Master and the Chaplain would then embrace him as they welcomed him into the Order.

The Templar administration would subsequently supply the new member with what were to be his only personal effects – he had to take great care of these items, as they did not belong to him. He was supplied with military equipment, similar to that which other knights of the time would have owned: body armour, a pair of iron grieves, a helmet with a nose-guard, a sword, a dagger, a spear, a large triangular shield, a white tunic and a saddle for his horse.

The remaining articles he was handed were: two sets of hose, two shirts, two pairs of breeches, a long loose gown, a heavy coat lined with sheepskin, a summer and a winter cloak, a tunic, a belt, a cotton and a felt cap, a towel, a razor, a bedsheet, a straw mattress, a couple of blankets, a napkin, two drinking glasses, a spoon and a table knife.

THE TEMPLAR CURSE

On 18 March 1314, the Grand Master Jacques de Molay and his comrade Charnay were burned on a slow fire, over a pyre erected on a small island on the River Seine. This island was known as the Island of Jews, and was situated in between the Church of the Hermit Brotherhood and the King's gardens. Before the purifying fire consumed his body, Jacques de Molay shouted a terrible prophecy at his executioners:

*God knows that I am going to die unjustly.
Because of this, misfortune will soon reach
those who have condemned us without
justice. God will avenge our deaths, I die
with that conviction. To you, my Lord, I
beg that you direct your gaze onto Our
Lady so that she gives us refuge.*

Next, he turned to face the King's
palace, and with a thundering roar he
exclaimed:

*Clement V, Pope, I summon you to appear before the Tribunal of God
within forty days and you, King Philip, within less than a year.*

On 20 April of that same year, Pope Clement V passed away as a
result of an intestinal infection, while staying at the Castle of Roquemaure
(perched above the Rhone Valley). Soon the monarch himself would
experience the same fate: on 4 November that year, Philip IV of France
suffered an apoplectic attack while he was riding his horse at Fontainebleu.
On the 29th, a little over nine months after having been cursed by de
Molay, Philip died.

But the Pope and the King were not the only ones cursed by de
Molay's words: none of their other accomplices or instigators of the trial
met a pleasant ending. Nogaret, the King's favourite, had taken an active
part in the trial of the Templar Knights, and also died in 1314, after having
fallen into disrepute. Esquieu de Floyran, a mischievous plotter who since
1304 had travelled the kingdoms of Christendom slandering the Templars,
was stabbed in mysterious circumstances in a street brawl, and also died
in 1314.

Templar renegades Bernard Pelet and Gerard de Laverna, who
had betrayed their Order brothers by making several accusations against
them, were hung by royal decree charged with numerous crimes. Later, on
30 April 1315, Enguerrand de Marigny, the finance minister and another of
the King's favourites, was charged with the embezzlement of public funds.
Lastly, when on 21 January 1793 the guillotine severed the head of Louis
XVI, an exalted spectator mounted the staging and, dipping his hands into
the dead king's blood, went on to splatter the crowd with it while at the
same time shouting: 'I baptize you, people, in the name of liberty and of
Jacques de Molay!' In response to this, part of the multitude passionately
exclaimed: 'Jacques de Molay has finally been avenged!'

FRAGMENT FROM THE ARREST ORDER OF 1307 AD

We have been informed by various persons worthy of our good faith of a bitter thing, a deplorable thing, a thing that is horrific to be thought about and terrifying to listen to, a detestable crime, an execrable villainy, an abominable act, an appalling infamy, something that is utterly inhuman or rather, foreign to all humanity.

This information has struck our ears and moved them with great astonishment and made us tremble with violent horror; and when we have weighed the gravity of it, an immense hurt has gradually begun to swell within us; a pain that has become even more cruel from the moment when there is no room left for doubt regarding the enormity of the crime, which overflows to the point of becoming an offence to the divine majesty, a disgrace to all humanity, a pernicious example of evil and a scandal of universal proportions. (...)

We have recently found out through information given to us by persons worthy of our good faith, that the Brothers of the Order of the Militia of the Temple are as wolves dressed as lambs; hiding behind the monastic habit of the Order, they have been miserably insulting the religion of our faith, crucifying in our days and once more Our Lord Jesus Christ, who had already been crucified to bring about the redemption of the human race, and showering him with injuries more grave than those he suffered when on the Cross.

When they enter the Order and take their vows, they are presented with his image and, horrible cruelty, they spit three times on his face, after which, stripped of the garments that they wore during their secular lives, naked, they are led into the presence of him who receives them [into the Order] or of his substitute and they are kissed by him, in accordance to the odious ritual of their Order, first on the lowest part of the backbone, second on the navel and third on the mouth, for the shame of human dignity.

And after having offended the divine law through pursuing such abominable paths and such detestable acts, they are forced by their sworn oath and without any fear of offending human laws, to abandon themselves to each other without denial, whenever they are required to do so, and due to the vice produced by a horrible and frightful concubinage.

THE TEMPLAR MYSTERIES

In parallel to the official history of the Knights Templar, we can trace a second historical dimension that is far more elusive and mysterious. With the disappearance of the Order, this alternative history of the Templars became even more clandestine and enigmatic.

Numerous orally transmitted legends and written accounts dating back to the Middle Ages report that, under the guise protecting pilgrims, the Templars were carrying out their real mission: to retrieve secret documents that lay undiscovered among the ruins of the Holy Land. Their mission lasted almost a whole decade, as they excavated among the rubble. Once they had found the documents, they returned to Europe with them. This alternative version of their history maintains that it was precisely these invaluable secret documents – guarded to this date by the Priory of Sion – that empowered the Templars in such a way. The level of international influence that the Templars attained (in such a short period) is difficult to

A knight being admitted to the Templar Order.

51

comprehend, yet this second version of events would better explain the mastery and dominion that they achieved. According to our second account of events, the secret texts they had discovered were the Sangreal documents, which trace the royal lineage and descendants of Christ.

Around the middle of the 12th century, a pilgrim named Johann von Wurzburg wrote a travel chronicle relating his visit to the so-called 'stables of Solomon', which were situated underneath the ruins of the Temple of Solomon (let us remind ourselves at this point that the official history of the Templars also states the fact that, as soon as they reached Jerusalem, the knights took lodgings in an edifice built upon the ruins of the Temple of Solomon). In von Wurzburg's account, as well as in various historical research papers, it is reported that the Solomon temple stables were sufficiently large to accommodate two thousand horses, and that the Templars performed excavations within them. At this point in time (the middle of the 12th century) the Order was in its early stages, and its numbers counted no more than nine members in total. The question that consequently ensues is: what were these nine Templar knights doing, when they were supposed to be looking after the safety of pilgrims, excavating within the ruins of King Solomon's ancient temple? The inevitable answer is that, without a shadow of a doubt, they were looking for something; supposedly it is what they found that allowed them to return to Europe in triumph a decade later, and what made them into one of the most powerful organizations of its time. But, what is it that they were looking for? And what is it that they uncovered? Up until the disappearance of their Order, the Knights Templar closely guarded the secret of what it was they had found, and where it was kept by them. Not even after suffering horrendous torture did they confess a word on the matter. Therefore, numerous scholars and researchers have presumed that the Templars found and guarded something extremely precious; something that had nothing to do with material treasure such as money or jewellery.

Although the members of the Order of the Poor Knights of Christ and the Temple of Solomon never confessed to the nature of their discovery, towards the end of the 12th century and the beginning of the 13th, several poems attributed to the Templars the mission of keeping guard over the Holy Grail. Further poetry works dating from the same period stated that the knights of the Order had unearthed a priceless treasure that could not be unveiled or even named, and which they were charged with protecting. But why were the Templars charged with finding and safeguarding the Holy Grail? The answer is that they had been entrusted with this mission by the Priory of Sion, the order that existed behind the Templars, and which subsists to the present date.

THE PRIORY OF SION

As already mentioned, this is the secret order that existed behind the Knights Templar. It has been known under several different names, but the *Prieuré de Sion* (Priory of Sion) is its best known title. Even after their Order was destroyed in the 14th century the Templars continued to exist; however, in sharp contrast to the fortunes suffered by its military front, the Priory of Sion – as it was a clandestine brotherhood – remained practically intact throughout. In spite of the numerous internal struggles – often bloody – that it suffered throughout the years, the Priory has orchestrated behind the scenes many of the most important events in Western history; and even today, it influences and participates in many international affairs of a high order, particularly on the European continent. The Priory of Sion has always been headed by Grand Masters, among whom we may find some of the most illustrious men in Western culture.

But let us start at the beginning. The Order of Sion was founded in Jerusalem in 1099 by the French monarch Godefroi de Bouillon, at the Prieuré du Notre Dame du Sion. Not much is known about this abbey, except that it was built by King Godefroi himself and that it served as shelter to the organization during its first years. From its early days, the Order already held considerable power (always behind the scenes, of course) and it has even been claimed that the monarchy of the Holy Land owed their throne to this enigmatic society.

In arround 1152, most of the Order of Sion members moved to France, subsequently going in different directions. Some of them moved into the great Priory of Saint-Samson in Orléans; others joined the Templar Order; a third group installed themselves at the 'small Priory of Mount Sion', situated in Saint Jean le Blanc, within the outskirts of Orléans. The city's municipal archives guard documents that certify that Louis VII had officially established the Order of Sion in Orléans. These same archives also hold a Papal bull from 1178, promulgated by Pope Alexander III, which confirms in an official manner the properties held by the Order in Spain, France, Italy and the Holy Land.

In 1188 (a year after the fall of Jerusalem), a second 'wave' of the Order of Sion members arrived in France from the Holy Land. On this same date, a definitive separation took place between the Knights Templar and the Priory Order members. The Priory largely placed the blame for the loss of the Holy Land on the Templar Order and, more specifically, on its current Grand Master, Gérard de Ridefort, who is accused of treason in the Priory documents. Gérard de Ridefort dragged the Templars into battle at the Horns of Hattin. This battle was an absolute disaster for the Crusaders and brought about the fall of Jerusalem. The Order of Sion moved to France, leaving the Templars to fend for themselves. The ultimate rupture in the relationship between the two orders was symbolized by the cutting down of an eight-hundred-year-old elm tree at the city of Gisors.

But the changes that occurred in 1188 went far beyond the separation of the two societies and the symbolic axing of an ancient elm tree. Until that year, both the Knights Templar and the Order of Sion had shared the same Grand Master. From 1188 on, the Order of Sion would select its own Grand Master, thus becoming completely separate from the Order of the Temple. According to the Priory documents, Jean de Gisors presided as the Priory of Sion's first Grand Master. He was born in 1133 and died in 1220. An extremely influential landowner an nobleman, de Gisors was also nominal lord to the fortress of Normandy, where the meetings between the kings of France and England took place.

A further change occurring that year was related to the Order's title: it changed its name from 'Order of Sion' to 'Priory of Sion'.

THE DA VINCI CODE'S GRAND MASTER:
HIS VISIBLE FACETS

Born in 1452 in the Italian region of Tuscany, Leonardo da Vinci constituted a paradigm of absolute genius. He personified the ultimate archetype of the all-encompassing Renaissance man: painter, sketch artist, sculptor, engineer, architect, inventor, musician, and philosopher. His enormous curiosity (the undeniable trigger to all of his achievements) manifested itself very early on in his life: as a child he used to sketch mythological animals of his own invention, inspired by a profound observation of the natural surroundings in which he grew up.

At the age of fourteen, he entered Andrea del Verrocchio's workshop as an apprentice. During his six years at Verrochio's workshop, da Vinci learnt the arts of painting and sculpture, as well as the techniques and mechanisms lying behind the visual arts. He then entered Antonio Pollaiuolo's workshop, where he was initiated in the study of anatomy; it is also presumed that this is where da Vinci first became acquainted with the study of Latin and Greek.

The earliest of his known commissioned works was the construction of a copper sphere designed by Brunelleschi to crown the church of Santa Maria del Fiore in Florence.

At the time, this metropolis was one of the wealthiest cities in Europe; it was also where the Medici family had established their court, which – in great part – owed its splendour to the numerous artists who inhabited it. Da Vinci became part of the Medici court; however, when he could not manage to obtain anything from Lorenzo de Medici but praises to his qualities as a courtier, he decided to look beyond Florence. At the age of thirty, he moved to Milan, where he presented himself to the powerful Ludovico Sforza. Sforza was an influential man in Milan, and da Vinci remained at his court for seventeen years. Although his main occupation there was as a military engineer, his projects (mostly unrealized) included painting, mechanics (he invented an innovative lever system to multiply human strength) and hydraulics. Using the work of

Leonardo da Vinci

Piero della Francesca and Leon Battista Alberti as his starting point, da Vinci began writing notes on the science of painting. At the same time, he also worked on designing and constructing lutes, on plans for the channelling of rivers and on ingenious defence systems against enemy artillery. In 1494, he created a series of drawings to accompany Luca Pacioli's (a mathematician and friend of da Vinci) treatise *Divina Proportione*. With these drawings, da Vinci proclaimed that the form and structure of objects should be unravelled and understood through attentive observation, so that they could be described through painting in the most exact manner possible. In this way, drawing became the most important instrument in da Vinci's didactic method: it can be said that in his notes, the text is there to explain the drawings, rather than the other way round. Due to this, Leonardo da Vinci is considered to be the inventor of modern scientific drawing.

Even though it does not seem that he was much concerned with forming his own school, his workshop in the city of Milan gradually generated a group of loyal pupils: Andrea Solari, Giovanni Boltraffio, etc. By the end of the 15th century, da Vinci started working on *The Madonna of the Rocks* and *The Last Supper*. The latter would become not only a celebrated Christian icon, but also the object of numerous pilgrimages from artists across the European continent.

When the French invaded Milan around 1499, Ludovico Sforza lost his power, and so da Vinci abandoned the city and moved to Venice. There he was hired as chief engineer working for the 'Signoria' of the city, which was at the time being threatened by Turkish forces. Within a few weeks of being in Venice, da Vinci had designed a series of projects that remained unrealized – in many cases – until the 19th and 20th centuries (among these were ships constructed with double walls to protect them from enemy fire, large pieces of artillery fitted with delayed action projectiles and a submarine meant for individual use). Because of various factors, none of these projects were built during his lifetime and, in April 1500, Leonardo da Vinci returned to Florence after twenty years' absence. Working once more as a military engineer, he was employed at the service of Cesare Borgia, who after a short time fell into disrepute and became ill. At this stage in his life, da Vinci was already hailed as one of the most important masters in Italy, holding claim to works such as (in addition to the ones already mentioned) *The Virgin and Child with St Anne*, *Leda and the Swan* and (the most celebrated artwork in the history of painting) *La Gioconda* or *The Mona Lisa*. The latter was famous from the moment of its creation, and is still today considered the definitive model for the creation of portraits. It is not known who originally commissioned this wonderful piece, yet we do know that its author sold it to King Francis I of France for the price of four thousand gold pieces. Among other factors, the Mona Lisa is famous for her enigmatic smile which, according to legend, was induced by the painter in his model through the sound of lutes.

Meanwhile, da Vinci's interest in scientific study gradually became more and more acute. He attended medical corpse dissections, and then used what he had learnt to create drawings describing the structure and functioning of the human body. He also made systematic observations on the flight of birds, guided in this by his steadfast conviction that man is also capable of flying. Years later, he returned to Milan when its French governor, Charles d'Amboise, offered him the post of architect and painter to the court. From 1515 onwards, da Vinci's health, which had been good up until that moment, started to deteriorate (among other things, his right arm became paralysed) and, on 2 May 1519, he died in the city of Cloux.

THE DA VINCI CODE'S GRAND MASTER:
HIS HIDDEN FACETS

Although it is not widely known, da Vinci had an esoteric side to his personality that influenced both his life and his works. His knowledge of the occult may be spotted in his paintings, as well as in a multiplicity of his manuscripts; full of coded thoughts and observations, these texts reveal his understanding of the enigmas of life and the universe...and of the true

nature of the relationship between Mary Magdalene and Jesus Christ, as well as – of course – the Holy Grail. As a member of the Priory of Sion, it is only natural that da Vinci was privy to all of this information.

Nowadays, bioenergetics has revealed that an individual's complete DNA is contained within a single cell; moreover, quantum physics confirms that the formation of the whole universe is printed on a single atomic particle. Da Vinci wrote 'this is the true miracle: that all forms, all images from every part of the Universe are contained within a single point' – this is a very similar statement to the one expounded by physicist David Bohm and the holonomic brain model he created. How could da Vinci perceive something that, only many centuries later, would be discovered by science (and only through the use of highly powerful technical instruments)?

On the other hand, the painter's esoteric interests have been confirmed and demonstrated. Numerous researchers characterise da Vinci as a sort of 'primitive Rosicrucian', while Giorgio Vasari (plastic artist and biographer, a contemporary of da Vinci) said that he had a 'heretical mentality'.

For example, in *The Last Supper*, the figure sitting directly on the right side of Jesus (a place of honour) is not a young man, but a young woman; to be more specific, it is Mary Magdalene. Several small details confirm this fact: the two figures are dressed as mirror images of each other; that is, Magdalene's robes constitute the inverted reflection of Christ's robes. In addition, Jesus and Magdalene are portrayed as being joined at the hip, leaning in opposite directions to form a sort of cone, a very similar shape to that of the symbol representing the female womb, a chalice, the Grail interpreted as a cup or receptacle. Furthermore, this occult symbolic representation appears towards the centre of the painting (obviously giving it a central character), yet it is slightly displaced towards the left (if we are facing the painting); the left side is associated with the feminine, while the right side is associated with the masculine. In addition, the jealousy and resentment felt by Peter towards Mary Magdalene, which are clearly outlined in the Gnostic Gospels, are also given representation in the mural: the apostle's hand is painted in a menacing gesture, seemingly threatening Magdalene's fragile neck as if it were a blade.

Examination of the underpainting of this work reveals that there might be two virtually identical Christ figures, in which case the painting could be working as a confession by da Vinci, who would be subscribing to an ancient 'sacrilegious' idea, according to which, Jesus had a twin brother.

In *The Madonna of the Rocks* (beyond the obvious reading of the painting as representing the Virgin Mary, Uriel, the infant Saint John the Baptist, and the infant Jesus searching for shelter in a cave) we may see further things; in particular, we may find the portrayal of 'unconventional' relationships between the different characters painted. In contrast to the usual scene in which Jesus blesses John, it is the infant John who is blessing Jesus this time. In addition, we can see Mary threatening John by holding her hand over his head. And lastly, just below Mary's curved fingers, Uriel is making a cutting gesture with his own hand, as if slicing the invisible head held by Mary's claw-like fingers.

Some of the symbols appearing in the Last Supper are based on the Gnostic Gospels.

In the *Mona Lisa*, the search for hidden symbols has been made more complex; it is not a case of sharpening our gaze and noting visual details; this time we are dealing with complex word play, such as the great Italian master used to love: in this instance, we need to combine the pagan past of ancient Egypt with da Vinci's Italian Renaissance reality. In fact, we may find that the concealed secret message of the painting in contained within its own title: Amon and Isis were one of ancient Egyptian mythology's most famous couples. Amon was the God of Fertility and Isis was his female counterpart. For a long time, the latter deity's pictogram was represented as L'ISA – so that the mythological couple's name was AMON L'ISA, a suspiciously familiar one to that of 'Mona Lisa'. Hence, the title of the painting becomes an allegorical anagram for the 'sacred spouses' archetype, representing the divine union of the masculine and the feminine. This latter aspect is additionally and notoriously reinforced by the androgyny of the famous image, which possesses one of the most enigmatic smiles in history.

THE HOLY GRAIL

As we mentioned earlier, the Holy Grail was the link uniting the Knights Templar and the Priory of Sion. *The Da Vinci Code* is devoted to the 'goal' they shared: to understand what the Holy Grail is and what it represents occupies a large part of the novel. As it is stated in the book:

The Holy Grail is probably the most sought after treasure of humanity. It has inspired legends, provoked wars and searches that have lasted several lifetimes.

But...what exactly is the Holy Grail? The truth is that this is not a simple question to answer.

The Grail is a mysterious and unattainable object, a far-reaching concept. According to certain traditions, it was the chalice from which Jesus and his disciples drank during the Last Supper. Others claim that it was the cup with which Joseph of Arimathea collected and kept the blood of the crucified Jesus Christ. John then took the cup with him to England; specifically, to Glastonbury. A third line of thought proclaims that both of these statements are true. Some versions confirm all of this, yet place Mary Magdalene in the position of Joseph of Arimathea. Through the years, the Grail has also been interpreted as being a stone fallen from the Heavens, a deposit for relics, a secret book, a heavenly manna and a table.

And, of course, royal blood materialized in a child, a concept that has always been concealed, and which *The Da Vinci Code* reveals. However, in order to get to the occult history of the Holy Grail, we must first inevitably look at its public history: for centuries, the Grail – whatever it might be – has made an appearance in literary works, in the songs of troubadours and in popular legends.

THE HOLY GRAIL ACCORDING TO ROMANCES

During the first millennium of our era, the absolute silence we encounter surrounding the Grail is of the utmost importance and interest. We find practically no texts of any kind (including poetic, narrative, historical and dramatic texts) that refer to its existence. It is only at the beginning of the 12th century that the Holy Grail starts to make an appearance within various writings. Of course, and as we shall see later on, this constitutes no casual date; on the contrary, this date is intimately linked to the two other protagonists of our current chapter: the Order of the Knights Templar and the Priory of Sion.

Grail romances (extensive narrative poems) were essentially based on pagan concepts referring to nature, the cycle of the seasons, birth, death, rebirth, etc. With the emergence of these romances, we find ourselves moving back towards the earlier cult of the Goddess and its ideology, rather than towards the prescriptive and orthodox Christian concepts that were imposed following the Council of Nicaea. Circulated mainly by oral transmission, the basic character of these early Grail romances was therefore pagan.

As we move forward into the Middle Ages, the idea of the Grail suffers a transformation, as it becomes generally regarded as a mystical relic linked to Jesus Christ. At this stage, the Holy Grail started to generate a great number of written romances; nevertheless, we still cannot trace in these texts a unanimous definition of what specifically the Holy Grail is.

The more ancient of these manuscripts date back to the 12th and 13th centuries, and emerged at the court of the Count of Champagne who, it is interesting to note, is presumed to have been the founder of the Templar Order. But this is by no means the single existing link between the Knights Templar and the romances of the Grail. In fact, the particular moment in time in which the Holy Grail romances flourished and reached cult status, coincides with the separation that took place between the Templar Order and the Order of Sion in 1188. Subsequently, and in unison with the loss of the Holy Land in 1291 and the dissolution of the Order of the Temple in 1307, the romances of the Grail disappeared from history's stage for about two centuries. However, Sir Thomas Malory would revive them in 1470 with his celebrated work *Le Morte d'Arthur*, and from that date onwards, the Holy Grail romances have occupied a pre-eminent position within Western culture.

But let us once more turn our attention to those earlier romances; those texts dating back to the 12th and 13th centuries. According to specialist scholars, the first authentic romance about the Grail dates from

1188; precisely the same year in which the Order of the Temple and the Order of Sion dissolved their association. This original Grail romance is titled *Le Roman de Perceval* or *Le Conte du Graal*. Its author was Chrétien de Troyes, a member of the court of Champagne, whose work constitutes a sort of prototype on which later variations of the story were to be based. The romance's text is mysterious, intriguing and open to multiple interpretations. Inevitably, these characteristics are enhanced by the fact that it was never completed: Chrétien de Troyes died in 1188, and it is unclear if he did so before finishing his romance or if he finished but there is no complete copy remaining. The latter is very probable, as the year Chrétien de Troyes died, and the members of theTemplar Order and of the Priory of Sion separated, the city of Troyes was set on fire. *Le Roman de Perceval* or *Le Conte du Graal* takes place at an indeterminate moment in time during the reign of King Arthur. Its protagonist is Percival or Perceval, who is described in the text as the 'Son of the Widowed Lady'. He abandons his mother and leaves in search of a knighthood. During his journey, Percival encounters an enigmatic fisherman – the 'Fisher King' – who invites him to spend the night at his castle; and it is during these particular circumstances that the Grail makes its appearance. The romance never explains exactly what the Grail is. In addition, this early version of the Grail story does not establish any links between the Grail (whatever it is) and Jesus Christ. Yet the Grail does appear, and it is made of gold and encrusted with precious jewels, and its carrier is a lady. Percival is unaware of the fact that he has been presented with the Grail so that he can ask the following question: 'who is served with it [the Grail]?' A highly ambiguous question if there ever was one... Percival does not ask the expected question and, on the following day, he awakens to find an empty and deserted castle. Further on in the tale, he is made aware of the consequences of having failed to ask the question: his oversight has been the cause of a disastrous misfortune befalling the world. Percival also discovers that he forms part of the 'family of the Grail', and that the mysterious fisherman was in fact his own uncle. Within an instant, and becuase of his experience with the Grail, Percival declares that he has stopped loving God, or that he has stopped believing in His existence.

With the passing of time, Chrétien de Troyes's subject matter would influence the creation of a multitude of other European literary productions; yet these other texts held certain characteristics that de Troyes's romance did not: basically, they linked the Grail story to King Arthur and to Jesus Christ.

One of these productions was the *Roman de l'estoire dou Saint Graal*, written by Robert de Boron presumably between 1190 and 1199.

The Knights Templar, custodians of the Holy Grail.

In this version of the story, the Grail has been fully transformed into a Christian symbol. De Boron alludes to it as the drinking cup that was used during the Last Supper, and later used by Joseph of Arimathea to collect the blood of Jesus when he was lowered from the Cross; and it is this sacred blood that which endows the Grail with its magical powers. De Boron's narrative goes on to relate how, after the Crucifixion, Joseph of Arimathea's family took the Grail into their care. For de Boron, the legends and romances regarding the Grail refer to the fortunes of Joseph's family. Due to this conviction, he states in his narrative that Galahad is the son of Joseph of Arimathea, and that the Grail falls into the hands of Jesus' son-in-law (Sir Brons), who subsequently takes it to England, and then becomes the Fisher King. In a similar manner to *Le Roman de Perceval* or *Le Conte du Graal*, de Boron's story describes Percival as the 'Son of the Widowed Lady'. However, in this second version, Percival is instead the Fisher King's grandson. Furthermore, in opposition to Chrétien de Troyes's romance, this version of the story does not take place during the era of King Arthur, but rather in the times of Joseph of Arimathea.

A further romance on the Grail is *Perlesvaus*. Composed by an anonymous author, it was written during approximately the same epoch as Robert de Boron's work, and so they have a lot in common.

This version of the Grail story takes place – like *Le Roman de Perceval* or *Le Conte du Graal* – in the age of King Arthur. Percival, a wanderer, arrives at a castle inhabited by a group of initiates to the Grail. He is received by two masters who, like the rest of their group, are dressed in white with a red cross on their chests. One of these masters asserts that he has personally seen the Grail and is familiar with Percival's lineage. During the course of the story, Percival is referred to as forming part of Joseph of Arimathea's family lineage. It has been conjectured that the anonymous author of *Perlesvaus* could have been a Templar Knight. This presumption is largely due to the extraordinarily detailed knowledge of military combat, including tactics and strategies, arms and armour in the text. We can find other details in the novel that are also fascinating. One of these is the abundance of elements linked to magic and alchemy that appears within the course of the text, as well as several allusions made that are of a pagan – or even heretical – nature, and which refer to the 'calumnies' spread regarding the Knights Templar and/or Gnostic thought. But what is the Grail described as within this third version of the tale? This is a rather complicated question to answer. In fact, in *Perlesvaus*, the Grail is purely a sequence of images or visions that may be interpreted as different things, or as different levels belonging to a single thing: a crowned and crucified king, a child, a man wearing a crown of thorns on his head and bleeding in various parts of his body, a non-specific manifestation and – lastly – a chalice. Several students of the text have pointed to the fact that, in reality, these different elements or visions constitute the metaphorical representation of a lineage, or of certain individuals belonging to that lineage. Finally, the text's images may (of course) also be read as the series of visions generated by some sort of Gnostic experience of illumination.

A fourth romance, *Parzival*, was composed between the years 1195 and 1216 by Wolfram von Eschenbach, and is considered to be the most famous and significant of the romances on the Holy Grail dating from this early period. This work possesses a practically endless richness and it has triggered any numbe of interpretations and commentaries throughout the centuries, making it impossible to detail them all within this single volume. What follows is a sort of summary of the different views existing on the text.

At the beginning of his book, the author states that Chrétien de Troyes's version of the Grail story is mistaken, while his own version is correct and can even be considered a sort of 'initiation document'. This, he admits, is due to the fact that his romance contains a secret hidden within its pages. He bases this claim on the assurance that he has received privileged information from a certain Kyot of Provence, who – in his turn – obtained it from a certain Flegetanis. Up until today, researchers have been unable to determine if these two characters really existed or if they were fictitious entities. In spite of this, it is generally presumed that Kyot of Provence was in fact Guiot de Provins, a troubadour monk who was a spokesperson for the Templar Order, and who visited Germany in 1184, where he could have easily met von Eschenbach.

As in earlier versions of the Grail story, Percival is also the protagonist of this tale. The custodians of the Grail and the family of the Grail are constituted by a number of Templar knights, who call to their service specific individuals. These individuals must in their turn be initiated into some sort of mystery, and are subsequently sent out to the world on a mission to represent the knights, do things in their name, and to sometimes occupy a throne. Most of the tale's narrative takes place in France, as the author assures us that Camelot – King Arthur's royal court – is at Nantes.

So, the question is: what is the Holy Grail in this version? What becomes clear after having attentively read the complete poem is that – for the author – the Grail does not simply constitute an object of gratuitous mystery; it is a sort of means to an end; a way of concealing something of transcendental importance. Page after page, von Eschenbach repeatedly urges its readers to unravel what is concealed in between the lines of his text, while at the same time constantly reiterating the compelling necessity of keeping the secret. And so, once again, the Grail is in this text something elusive and vague. At times in the narrative it appears to be a kind of horn of plenty, yet one of Percival's uncles mentions that it has the capacity of transforming itself into something far more powerful: a stone endowed with miraculous powers, such as bestowing some sort of eternal youth on its owner: 'such is the power that the stone gives a man, that his flesh and bones rapidly become youthful once more.' The experts have reached

Parzival, one of the many romances that narrate the story of the Holy Grail.

different interpretations regarding this 'Grail stone', which is also referred to as *'lapsit exillis'*: this could be a deformation of *'lapsit ex caelis'*, that is, 'it fell from the Heavens', or a corrupt version of the expression *'lapsis elixir'*, term referring to the fabulous Philosopher's Stone relentlessly sought after by alchemists. In addition, the concept of a stone carries a high level of symbolism in Christian terms: within the New Testament, Jesus Christ is equated with 'the angular stone forgotten by builders', while Peter is the 'stone' or 'rock' on which Christ builds his Church.

A SECOND HOLY GRAIL, THE TRUE ONE?

The idea of the Grail constituting the bloodline of Jesus Christ and the origins of his family lineage is more recent than the concepts we mentioned in the last section. Although – of course – both the Knights Templar and the Priory of Sion have known about this idea for centuries (as does the Church, which tries to conceal it) and members have revealed their concealed knowledge through works of art, the truth is that not until practically contemporary times have scholars and researchers finally reached this same conclusion.

However, we must not presume that the interpretations we mentioned earlier regarding the Grail must necessarily be set against the above one. For example, some of the earlier stories and readings of the Holy Grail, such as it being the cup that collected the blood of Jesus Christ, can well be understood metaphorically. A metaphor, an allegory, a veiled symbol standing for something much more powerful – if this were possible – to gather and hold the blood of Jesus could, in this instance, symbolize the gathering and guarding of his royal blood materialized in a child (a daughter, in fact) and in all of his descendants.

And all of this knowledge concerning the Grail is brought together in a set of priceless secret documents: the Sangreal documents, a compilation of chronicles that narrate the time spent by Mary Magdalene in France, including the birth of her daughter Sarah, the history of her descendants and her complete family tree. But this is not the only information that the Sangreal documents contain (although this is quite a lot already). The Sangreal library also holds tens of thousands of pages of documentation that precede Emperor Constantine's era (and therefore precede the Council of Nicaea) and talk about that human Jesus Christ we referred to in our initial chapter. These early texts constitute what are known as the 'Purist Documents'. Furthermore, an unconfirmed hypothesis even states that the 'Purist Documents' contain manuscripts written by Jesus himself. And it was precisely this extremely valuable documentary treasure that the Knights Templar uncovered at Solomon's Temple, and subsequently brought with them to Europe.

But the Knights Templar had not only been entrusted with the search for these documents. Together with the Sangreal texts, they also found the tomb containing the mortal remains of Mary Magdalene. The Templars' journey was therefore, above all, a pilgrimage to pray at the feet of the lost and concealed female divinity.

The Holy Grail is then in reality two things at the same time. On the one hand, it is the lineage and descendants of Jesus Christ; the Royal Blood, whose custody was entrusted to the knights of the Order of the Temple (an order created by the Priory of Sion). On the other hand, the Holy Grail is also – literally – the receptacle that received and held the blood of Jesus, that is, the womb of Mary Magdalene and – by extension – Mary Magdalene herself.

CHAPTER 3

THE PRIORY
OF SION, FROM
THE 12TH
CENTURY
TO THE
PRESENT
DAY

THE PRIORY OF SION, FROM THE 12TH CENTURY TO THE PRESENT DAY

In the previous chapter we dealt with the early history of the Holy Grail, as well as with that of the Knights Templar and the Priory of Sion. So, what happened to both of these orders after the Middle Ages?

The Knights Templar, who were the Priory's armed front and acted openly, were practically exterminated, although not completely. Today, various organizations purport to belong to the Order, as for example the '*Ordo Supremus Militaris Temply Hierosolymitani*' (formed by knights from Argentina, Colombia, Chile, Uruguay and the United States), the 'Rovers' (in Mexico) and the Court of Templar Knights of Sul de Minas.

Isaac Newton (left), Wolfgang Amadeus Mozart (above right), and Victor Hugo (below right), three of the Priory of Sion's Grand Masters.

Concealed at all times (although not so much so from 1956 onwards, as we shall see further on in the book), the Priory of Sion currently holds the mission of protecting the Sangreal documents, the tomb of Mary Magdalene and the lineage of Jesus Christ, that is, the Merovingian dynasty that is still to be found among us today.

But...how did *La Prieuré de Sion* survive from its origins to the early 21st century?

Throughout the centuries, and as we shall be able to appreciate further on in the text, the Priory's existence was led in a clandestine manner, behind the scenes, and with the presence of an important man (or an important woman) occupying the post of Grand Master. In general, and as can be seen in the list that follows, all Grand Masters either had links to the political powers of their time, belonged to a secret society, were privy to alchemical mysteries or were renowned artists...and sometimes were even several of these things at once.

THE PRIORY OF SION AND ITS GRAND MASTERS

Within the illustrious gallery of Grand Masters of the Priory of Sion we may find essential personages in the history of humanity. What now follows is a complete list of the Priory's Grand Masters, from Jean de Gisors to the latest known Grand Master, French writer Jean Cocteau.

BRIEF BIOGRAPHICAL NOTES ON THE GRAND MASTERS

Jean de Gisors: the first independent Grand Master of the Priory of Sion. He was born in 1133 and died in 1220.

Marie de Saint-Clair: she was born around 1192 in Scotland. Marie de Saint-Clair was a descendant of Henri de Saint-Clair, Baron of Rosslyn, who accompanied Godefroi de Bouillon during the First Crusade. Some non-conclusive evidence indicates that, in addition, she could have been the second wife of Jean de Gisors.

Guillaume de Gisors: he was Jean de Gisors' grandson, and was born in 1219. Little is known about him except for the fact that he was initiated into the Order of the Ship and the Order of the Double Crescent in 1269 (both of these orders were created by Louis IX for the nobles who accompanied him on the ill-fated Sixth Crusade).

GRAND MASTERS

The following listing forms part of the so-called
Dossiers Secrets, which were discovered at the
Bibliotéque Nationale de Paris.

Jean de Gisors	1188-1220
Marie de Saint-Clair	1220-1266
Guillaume de Gisors	1266-1307
Edouard de Bar	1307-1336
Jeanne de Bar	1336-1351
Jean de Saint-Clair	1351-1366
Blanche d'Evreux	1366-1398
Nicolas Flamel	1398-1418
René d'Anjou	1418-1480
Iolande de Bar	1480-1483
Sandro Botticelli	1483-1510
Leonardo da Vinci	1510-1519
Connétable de Bourbon	1519-1527
Ferdinand de Gonzague	1527-1575
Louis de Nevers	1575-1595
Robert Fludd	1595-1637
Johannes Valentinus Andreae	1637-1654
Robert Boyle	1654-1691
Isaac Newton	1691-1727
Charles Radclyffe	1727-1746
Charles de Lorraine	1746-1780
Maximillian de Lorraine	1780-1801
Charles Nodier	1801-1844
Victor Hugo	1844-1885
Claude Debussy	1885-1918
Jean Cocteau	1918-1963

Edouard de Bar: he was born in 1302, and was the Count de Bar. He was also the grandson of King Henry I of England, and the nephew of King Edward II. It is also highly probable (yet it has not been confirmed) that he was related to the Merovingian monarchy. When his daughter married, she joined the House of Lorraine, so from then onwards the genealogies of Bar and Lorraine have intermingled. Edouard de Bar took part in battles and military operations and purchased the Stenay estate for one of his uncles, Jean de Bar. He died in 1336 when he was shipwrecked near the Cypriot coast. According to the Priory documents, Edouard de Bar occupied his post as Grand Master to the Order at the early age of five; if this is true, it is possible that his uncle, Jean de Bar, acted for him until he came of age. Giving a minor the title of Grand Master is supposedly linked to hereditary ties or blood descent (let us remind ourselves of his possible family link to the Merovingian dynasty, mentioned earlier).

Jeanne de Bar: Edouard de Bar's eldest daughter. She was born in France in 1295 and died in London in 1261. At the age of fifteen she married the Count of Warren, Surrey, Sussex and Strathern. She divorced him after a few years. It seems that she enjoyed a very good relationship with the English throne, as well as with the French one; this enabled her to live in one country or the other, depending on personal and political circumstances. It is presumed that she was the sole Priory Grand Master to have relinquished her post, as she held the title only up until ten years prior to her death.

Jean de Saint-Clair: born around 1332, but does not seem to have been a truly notable character. The fact that somebody so 'insignificant' has occupied the post of Grand Master has brought scholars to the realization that – at that date – the Priory's highest office circulated exclusively among a web of inter-linked families.

Blanche d'Evreux: born in 1332, she was in fact Blanca de Navarra, the daughter of the King of Navarre. She died in 1398. She inherited the counties of Longueville and Evreux (adjacent to that of Gisors) from her father, and married Philip IV of France. According to various legends, she was involved in the science of alchemy, and there were even rumours regarding the existence of laboratories within her castles. It was also reported that she protected Nicolas Flamel.

Nicolas Flamel: Flamel was a famous French alchemist living during the 15th century. No confirmed dates exist regarding his birth and death, yet it is believed that he was born in 1330 near Pontoise, and that he died in 1418. His name is the first on the list of Grand Masters that holds no blood ties with the family genealogies appearing in the Priory documents. Although he came from a humble family background, Flamel managed to receive the education of a man of letters. Among his most celebrated writings we may find the following works: *Alchemical Studies* and *The Desired Desire / Janus Lacinius Therapus: Formula and Method to Perfect Vile Metals*; yet the text that is considered to be his capital work is *The Book of Hieroglyphic Figures*. The latter constitutes the most famous of all Western texts on alchemy, and it was written in order to shed new light on the subject matter of the 'Elixir of Life'. According to expert scholars on the history of alchemy, Flamel could have based his book on *The Sacred Book of Abraham the Jew*: Abraham was a prince, a priest, a Levite, an astrologer, and a philosopher. He originated from that tribe of Jewish people who, because of the wrath of God, were dispersed across Gallic lands. Abraham then wrote one of the most celebrated works within universal esoteric tradition. It is said that the original manuscript was deposited at the Arsenal library in Paris.

René d'Anjou: born in 1408. He became the Grand Master of Sion in 1418, at the age of ten, and so it was his uncle Louis, the Cardinal de Bar, who acted as Grand Master of his behalf for several years until he became old enough. René d'Anjou was an extremely important man during his lifetime, and as an example of this we can list the titles that he possessed: King of Hungary, King of Naples and Sicily, King of Aragon, Valencia, Majorca and Sardinia, King of Jerusalem, Count de Bar, Count of Piedmont, Count of Guise, Count of Provence, Duke of Anjou, Duke of Calabria and Duke of Lorraine. The title of King of Jerusalem – even though it was a purely nominal one – seems to point to a continuous line dating back to Godefroi de Bouillon. In 1445, one of Anjou's daughters married Henry VI of England.

Iolande de Bar: One of René d'Anjou's daughters. She was born in 1428. In 1445 she married Ferri, Lord of Sión-Valdemont. Following her husband's death, Iolande spent most of her lifetime at Sión-Valdemont. Under her patronage, the area went from being a centre of local pilgrimage to a sacred place for the entire Lorraine region. Subsequently, her son René became the Duke of Lorraine and, under his parents' instructions, went to Florence to receive an education. His teacher there was Georges Antoine Vespucci, who was one of Sandro Botticelli's principal patrons and protectors.

A detail from Botticelli's painting *The Birth of Venus*.

Sandro Botticelli: he was christened Alessandro di Mariano di Vanni Filipepi, and was born in Florence (it is not certain if the date was 1444 or 1445). During his early youth he worked as a goldsmith, although in the early 1460s he abandoned this profession for good in order to dedicate himself fully to the art of painting. He was one of Filippo Lippi's disciples, a Florentine artist of great renown. The particular style in which Lippi portrayed his Madonnas notably influenced the young Botticelli. Botticelli received his first commission in 1470: he was assigned the painting of a figure from the Fortaleza, which would integrate a series of seven virtues adorning the assembly chamber of the Corporation of Merchants. During his lifetime, Botticelli was a successful painter who worked at the Medici court. However, from 1490 onwards he began to decline, and he died in solitude in 1510. His most celebrated work is, without a doubt, *The Birth of Venus*, in which we can see the Goddess of Love being born from the foam created by the sea waves, after it has been fertilized by the skies. This magnificent work of art has received varying interpretations. Some consider it to be a symbolic representation of a helpless humanity in wait of the rebirth of God through Baptism. For other scholars, the Goddess of Love personifies the ideal of Truth, which, within Platonic doctrine, is identified with the ideal of Beauty. And, of course, this masterpiece can also be viewed as a representation of the birth of one of the greatest of goddesses.

Although it was believed for a long time that Botticelli was not involved in esoteric thought or in occultism, recent studies regarding the Renaissance period – such as, for example, works by Edgar Wind and Frances Yates – associate the painter with esotericism and, as in Leonardo da Vinci's case, believe that many of his works may be read through the use of a sort of 'secret code'. For example, his famous work, *Primavera* (*Spring*) can be read as being, among many other things, an extension on the theme of Arcadia and the underground current of esotericism.

Leonardo da Vinci: see chapter 2.

Connétable de Bourbon: he was born in 1490, and died in 1527. De Bourbon was probably one of the most powerful French lords during the early 16th century. He was the son of Claire de Gonzaga and his youngest sister married the Duke of Lorraine, who, in his turn, was the grandson of Iolande de Bar and the great grandson of René d'Anjou. De Bourbon was also the Viceroy of Milan, a city where he became acquainted with Leonardo da Vinci.

Ferdinand de Gonzague: he was better known as Ferrante de Gonzaga. De Gonzague was the son of the Duke of Mantua and of Isabella d'Este, and was born in 1507. His main title was that of Count of Guastalla. De Gonzague helped his cousin – Charles de Montpesier et Bourbon – in his military operations, and was also associated with François de Lorraine, the Duke of Guise, who was a pretender to the throne of France. In addition, he was one of Leonardo da Vinci's most fervent protectors, as well as being assiduously devoted to esotericism. The circumstances enveloping his death are extremely imprecise: one of the existing versions states that he died in Brussels in 1557; on the other hand, and according to the Priory of Sion documents, that was only the date in which he decided to go into hiding and, in this way, he continued to preside over the Order until his death in 1575.

Louis de Nevers: he was born in 1539. He held the title of Duke of Nevers, and was in fact Louis de Gonzaga, Ferrante de Gonzaga's nephew. Through family ties – whether blood ties or political ones – he was linked to the Hapsburg family and to the House of Lorraine. Among other things, and as the rest of the Gonzaga family, Louis de Nevers was deeply and fervently immersed in the tradition and practices of esotericism, and it is believed that he went into partnership with Giordano Bruno and John Dee, the most prominent English esoterist of his time.

Robert Fludd: he was the medical and philosophical exponent of Hermetic thought, as well as of other secret disciplines. Fludd was born in 1574, and died in 1637. In order to pursue the study of medicine, he abandoned his native England and left for France. There he became familiar with the secret doctrines of the arcane sciences, later on travelling to Spain, Italy, and Germany, country where he became associated with Janus Gruter, a friend of Johann Valentin Andreae. In order to cure his patients, Fludd used what he termed 'magnetic induction', which was in reality the use of his innate powers of healing. In his philosophical writings, he attributed fundamental importance to what he called 'the mystery of the

Light'; according to Fludd, those individuals that were able to get to know the Light and enter into it would be blessed with the knowledge of immortality. Fludd wrote and published numerous works regarding a multiplicity of esoteric subjects, while he developed some of the most complete formulations ever written regarding esoteric philosophy. He ascended to a highly prestigious post within the Royal Medical College in London. In addition, he formed part of the conclave of experts that presided over the translation of the Bible commissioned by James I, and he enjoyed the favours of both that king and his son Charles I.

Johannes Valentinus Andreae: he was a philosopher and an alchemist. Andreae was born in 1586 in Wurttemberg, and died in 1654. He wrote *The Reformation of Everybody*, a work that dealt with the subject matter of reformation from a moral, political, scientific and religious point of view, and whose target audience was all of the educated and sovereign men of Europe. Although the fact has never been confirmed, it was rumoured that Andreae formed part of a secret society of esoteric and Hermetic initiates. Without a doubt, his most celebrated work is *The Chymical Wedding of Christian Rosencreutz*, in which he ridicules the large number of impostors and adventurers who want to pass for alchemists.

Robert Boyle: a physician and chemist of Irish origins, Boyle was born into a large aristocratic family in 1624. Among his many important contributions, we can cite his improvement of the pneumatic machine, and his discovery that it is possible to store gases, accompanied by the formulation of a rudimentary theory on this discovery, which he subsequently followed with his definitive proposal, still known as Boyle's Law. Boyle also had an esoteric and alchemical side. He believed in the transmutation of gold and, during a stay in Geneva, he also became interested in diverse esoteric disciplines – including that of demonology. He was a great friend of Isaac Newton and John Locke, with whom he would get together in order to discuss science and alchemy. With the passing of time, he became increasingly interested in religious questions, writing several essays on the subject. In 1680, he was elected a member of the Royal Society. He died in 1691 and, just before his death, he handed over to his two friends (Newton and Locke) samples of a mysterious red powder; a substance that featured prominently within a large part of his correspondence, and within the annotations to his chemical experiments.

Isaac Newton: born in England in 1642, Newton was the father of mechanics and optics; he developed the 'method of fluxions', invented differential calculus, established the binomial theorem, explained the physical nature of colour and light, verified the theory of universal gravitation, and established the existing compatibility between his own law and Kepler's three laws on planetary motion. In 1687, Newton published his celebrated collection of works *Philosophiae Naturalis Principia Mathematica*: three volumes containing the fundamentals of physics and astronomy written in the language of pure geometry. Around this time of extremely fertile intellectual production, he had his first encounter with Robert Boyle. He subsequently formed a partnership

The altar in memory of Isaac Newton at Westminster Abbey, one of the most active centres in England.

with John Locke and an enigmatic individual named Nicholas Fatio de Duillier, who it seems, had been a spy working against Louis XIV of France. Their partnership was to last ten years. Newton defended the rights of the University of Cambridge against the unpopular King James II. When the king was dethroned and forced into exile, Newton was elected a Member of Parliament as a just reward for the effectiveness with which he had defended the University. He kept his seat in Parliament during several years, yet he was not very active during debates. In 1689, he started to work on The Chronology of Ancient Kingdoms, Amended – a study of ancient monarchies. In it, he tried to establish the origins of the institution of monarchy, as well as the primacy of Israel over other ancient cultures. He claimed all of this on the basis of a divine knowledge that he proclaimed to have possessed at one time, yet that had subsequently been corrupted and diluted. One of the basic theses of this volume was that, in spite of the loss and dissolution of his divine knowledge, something of this had filtered through time to reach Pythagoras, whose 'music of the spheres' was interpreted by Newton as a metaphor for his own law of gravity. As many other Masons did, Newton attributed great importance to the dimensions and configuration of Solomon's Temple, which – it was presumed – contained alchemical formulas. He was elected a member of the Royal Society in 1703 and, more or less around that same time, he struck up a friendship with a young French refugee, Jean Desaguliers, who was one of the men in charge of experiments at the Royal Society, and would years later become one of the principal figures responsible for the proliferation of Freemasonry in Europe. There is no evidence that Newton was a Mason, yet we do know for certain that he was a member of a partly Masonic institution named 'Spalding Gentlemen's Society'. Equally, some of his attitudes reflected opinions shared by the Masons of his time (such as, for example, to hold Noah in greater esteem than Moses, and to view him as a fountain of esoteric wisdom). During the last thirty years of his life, Newton practically abandoned his scientific investigations, and gradually confined himself to the study of religion, in particular, to some rather 'unorthodox' opinions. Newton deplored the idea of the Holy Trinity, and questioned the divinity of Jesus. He collected documents on the latter subject that would prove the idea of a human Jesus Christ. He also doubted the absolute authenticity of the New Testament. He died in 1727, and is buried at Westminster Abbey, among other great English gentlemen.

Charles Radclyffe: he was born in 1693. His mother was the illegitimate daughter of Charles II and his lover Moll Flanders. Radclyffe was also the cousin of the 'Young Pretender' (Charles Edward Stewart or Bonnie Prince Charlie), and of George Lee, Count of Lichfield. Radclyffe spent a large part of his life serving the cause of his House, the Stewarts. He was executed in 1746.

Charles de Lorraine: he was born in 1712. In 1744, he married Mary Anne, the sister of Austrian Empress Maria Theresa. The same year, he was named governor general of the Austrian Netherlands (what is today Belgium) and commander-in-chief of the Austrian army. Although he was defeated by Frederick the Great at the Battle of Leuthen in 1757, Charles de Lorraine was one of the most important and brilliant military men of his time. After the defeat, Empress Maria Theresa removed him from his post, and so he retired to Brussels. There he became a patron of the arts, gathering around him a brilliant court. In 1761, he became Grand Master of the Teutonic Order, which was a remnant of the Teutonic Knights, Germanic protégées of the Knights Templar. De Lorraine died in 1780.

Maximillian de Lorraine: he was born in 1756 and was Empress Maria Theresa's son and Charles de Lorraine's favourite nephew. Because of an accident that stopped him pursuing a military career, Maximillian dedicated his full energy to the Church. In 1784, he was named Bishop of Munster and Archbishop and Imperial Elector of Cologne. In 1780, when his uncle Charles died, Maximillian became the Grand Master of the Teutonic Order in his place. He was a tolerant and intelligent ruler, loved by his people, as well as a patron of the arts. Among his list of protégées we can find Haydn, Mozart and Beethoven. It is also widely suspected that he belonged to a Freemasonic association. He died in 1801.

Charles Nodier: he was born in 1780. Nodier was the son of a lawyer who, prior to the French Revolution, had been a member of a Jacobite society, and had also been a much esteemed Master Mason. Nodier was a precocious and highly prolific writer. His work covers a wide spectrum; within his fictional work we can find a voluminous collection of novels and within his non-fictional writings, we encounter essays on literature, travel chronicles, studies on painting, psycho-sociological research regarding the nature of suicide, esotericism, etc. Although he was sympathetic to the revolution, Nodier was not keen on Napoleon: he wrote and published works dismissing him, and was involved in conspiracies against him twice (in the years 1804 and 1812). He died in 1844.

Victor Hugo: he was born in 1802, the son of a French army officer. Victor Hugo studied in Paris and, at the age of fifteen, the French Academy of Arts awarded him a prize for one of his works of poetry. He was a writer of great renown during his own time (as well as in the history of universal literature), and achieved great success with works such as *Hernani* and *The Hunchback of Notre Dame*; yet his most successful work has to be *Les Miserables*. At a very early age, he became a fervent disciple of Charles Nodier and, together with his brother and Nodier, founded a publishing house in 1819. In 1825, Hugo, Nodier and their respective wives left together on a long journey to Switzerland. From the religious point of view, Victor Hugo was a deeply spiritual man, yet his opinions were not very orthodox. He repudiated the divinity of Jesus Christ, and was also an antitrinitarian. In large part due to Nodier's influence, he became highly and profoundly interested in questions related to esotericism and Gnostic thought, and this can be traced in his literary work. From the political point of view, he held complex (and even contradictory) opinions, yet it can be said that he had mostly monarchic ideals. He died in 1885.

Claude Debussy: he was born in 1862. Debussy was the founder of the so-called Symbolist school of music. His family origins were of a humble sort, yet his precocious genius allowed him – from a very early age – to come into contact with rich and influential people. As a teenager he worked as a pianist at the castle of the French President's lover. Later on, he travelled extensively in Russia, Italy and Switzerland, which allowed him to become acquainted with eminent people in a large part of Europe. Among his acquaintances were Victor Hugo, Paul Verlaine, Marcel Proust, André Gide, Oscar Wilde, and Paul Valéry. Debussy formed part of Symbolist circles, which at that time dominated French cultural life, and within these he was introduced to notable personages linked to Hermetic thought and magic. His close ties with esoteric questions can be appreciated in his work. Among his most celebrated compositions is the opera *Pelléas et Mélisande*, which is based on a play written by symbolist playwright Maurice Maeterlinck. Just before he died in 1918, Debussy had been working on an opera libretto based on the occultist play *Axel de Villiers de l'Isle-Adam*.

Jean Cocteau: he was born in 1889, and died in 1963. Cocteau possessed a multi-faceted artistic personality, working in many different artistic fields, such as the cinema, literature and painting. Among his literary production, the following works stand out: *Les Enfants Terribles* (a novel), and *The Eagle with Two Heads* (a play). As a filmmaker, he is mostly remembered for *The Beauty and the Beast* and *The Blood of a Poet*. Cocteau came from a family circle that was close to power, and who was prominent within the political arena; in addition, his uncle was an important diplomat. During the course of his life, Cocteau never distanced himself completely from these influential spheres. His works are – in general – laden with obscure symbolist references.

1956 AND PIERRE PLANTARD DE SAINT-CLAIR

The year that gives this section its title was a sort of punctuation mark in the history of the Priory of Sion. Although the Priory had worked in a surreptitious manner for many centuries, from 1956 onwards the Order's name appears recorded in the *Journal Officiel*, a weekly listing published by the French government in which all groups, organizations, and societies existing in the country must be declared. However...the Priory of Sion appears listed strictly as a research study association that provides its members with mutual aid and support. The association is based upon twenty-one statutes, yet these do not clarify what the Priory's objectives are, nor do they offer any indication regarding the organization's possible influence or sphere of interest.

Its members are classified according to seven categories, forming a traditional pyramidal hierarchical structure. At the pyramid's pinnacle is the Grand Master or 'Nautonnier'. The category immediately beneath the Grand Master is that of 'Prince Noachite de Notre Dame', followed by that of 'Croisé de Saint-Jean'. In descending order, the Priory's ladder continues with the 'Commandeurs', the 'Chevaliers', the 'Ecuyers', and – within the last category – the 'Preux'.

The question that springs to mind is: is this really a research study association that provides mutual aid between its members? Do its manifest objectives constitute a mere façade that conceal its true mission? A mission that has remained the same for many centuries: to protect the lineage of Jesus and the documents that confirm and explain it, as well as to help the descendants of the Merovingian dynasty (when the occasion is right) to return to the throne? So that we are able to answer these questions, we must first of all refer to an intriguing news article that originally appeared in January 1981 in the French press:

Pierre Plantard de Saint-Clair, the Priory of Sion's Grand Master from 1981 to 1984.

A real secret society consisting of 121 dignitaries, the Priory of Sion, founded by Godfrey of Bouillon in Jerusalem in 1099, has counted among its grand masters with individuals such as Leonardo da Vinci, Victor Hugo, and Jean Cocteau. This order held a convention in Blois, on the 17th of January of 1981 (the previous convention took place in Paris, on the 5th of June of 1956).

As a result of the convention recently held in Blois, Pierre Plantard de Saint-Clair was elected as Grand Master of the Order by 83 votes out of a total of 92 during the third voting.

This election of a Grand Master implies a decisive step in the evolution of the conception and spirit of the order regarding the outside world: this is due to the fact that the 121 dignitaries of the Priory of Sion are all distinguished members of the high-ranking financial world and of political and philosophical international societies, and Pierre Plantard is the direct descendant, through Dagobert II, of the Merovigian kings. The parchments of Queen Blanche of Castile, uncovered by Abbott Saunière in his church at Rennes-le-Chateau in 1891, have lawfully confirmed Plantard's royal lineage.

The Priory of Sion claims that it is in possession of the treasures from Solomon's Temple, beneath the Church of the Holy Sepulchre.

In 1956, the priest's niece sold these documents to Captain Roland Stanmore and Sir Thomas Frazer, and they were stored in a safety deposit box at Lloyds Bank Europe Ltd in London.

Is it not too much of a 'coincidence' that a humble research association dedicated to the mutual aid of its members, would specifically elect as its Grand Master a descendant of the Merovingian dynasty? Could it not be true that the Priory of Sion holds a series of ultimate goals that exceed simple study and mutual aid? In order to shed some light on this particular question, we will need to refer to the declarations made by Mr Plantard in 1973, when a French magazine published a transcript of a telephone conversation with him. All of his answers were elusive, cryptic, and, all in all, highly suggestive and created more questions than answers.

When Mr Plantard was specifically asked about the Priory's objectives, he replied the following:

That I cannot answer. The society that I belong to is exceedingly ancient. I limit myself simply to succeed others who have gone before me, to be a point along a line. We are custodians of certain things. And without any publicity.

So what is the Priory of Sion guarding so carefully and why do they not want any publicity? According to all that we have been expounding in this book, the answer can only be one: what the Priory is guarding so secretly is the bloodline of Jesus Christ, the Sangreal.

On the other hand, Jean-Luc Chaumeil, who interviewed Mr Plantard for a magazine, and who was engaged in extensive research on the subject of the Priory of Sion, holds a further opinion on the matter. He believes that the statutes presented by the Priory organization before the police were forged, and that, in reality, the Order holds ambitious political plans for the not very distant future. According to Mr Chaumeil, within a few years, a spectacular change is going to befall the French government; a political transformation that will lay down the path for a future monarchy of a social nature, with a Merovingian governor at its head. Orchestrating this political change, and working behind the scenes, will be the Priory of Sion (just as they have been responsible for numerous other momentous social changes throughout the years).

In 1979, Pierre Plantard gave the BBC an interview. His interviewers declared that although the final recorded conversation did not include any clear statements regarding the Priory's future plans, during the conversation that they had off-camera, Mr Plantard made abundant indirect remarks and insinuations. For example, he confessed to the fact that the Priory of Sion members were the guardians of the lost treasure of the Temple of Jerusalem. In addition, he insisted that the treasure's true nature was of a spiritual character, and led the interviewers to understand that this spiritual treasure partly consisted of a secret.

He also alluded to the fact that this secret would facilitate the occurrence of an important social change: the transformation of the existing French governmental institutions, which would, in its turn, lead the way to the restoration of monarchy.

THE RENNES-LE-CHATEAU MYSTERY

The church at Rennes-le-Chateau is not just the place where the secret parchments confirming the Merovingian ascendancy of Pierre Plantard de Saint-Clair were uncovered. In fact, the church is an esoteric centre, and its rich history includes the following: a legendary treasure, desecrated tombs, a church consecrated to Mary Magdalene, members of the Priory of Sion implicated in its history, a Templar ghost, a statue of Asmodeus holding the baptismal font and the possibility of finding the relics of Jesus Christ hidden somewhere within the church itself.

Rennes-le-Chateau is a small village atop the cliffs of a craggy mountain situated in the French region of Razès, about five kilometres from Couiza and forty kilometres from Carcassone.

In 1885, Father Bérenger Saunière arrived at Rennes-le-Chateau church. Consecrated to Mary Magdalene in 1059, the church had been built on top of a Visigothic structure dating back to the 6th century. At the time of Saunière's arrival, the temple was in a deplorable state of preservation. Because of this, in 1891, the priest decided to start working on its restoration. During the course of his construction work, the altar stone was removed, and Saunière discovered that it had been lying on top of two hollow columns. Within one of the columns, Father Saunière found several lacquered wooden cylinders that protected a set of four parchments. Two of these parchments constituted genealogies related to the Merovingian dynasty; one of them dating from 1244, and the other from 1644. The other two parchments had been produced in around 1780 by Abbott Antoine Bigou, who was the Rennes-le-Chateau parish priest at the time. Abbott Bigou had also been the chaplain of the aristocratic family of Blanchefort, whose ancestors had been linked to the Knights Templar; specifically to Bertrand de Blanchefort, who presided over the warrior monks as Grand Master of the Knights of the Order of the Temple around the middle of the 12th century.

The two parchments dating from Bigou's time appeared to be pious texts written in the Latin language, extracts from the New Testament. Yet this hypothesis was not fully convincing. The documents were formatted, to say the least, in a mysterious way: the words within the first parchment were linked in an incoherent manner, without any space lying in between them; in addition, a certain number of unnecessary letters had been inserted into the text. In the second parchment, the sentences ended in any which way, without any type of uniform criteria; also, certain letters were lifted above others. Researchers and scholars finally managed to decipher a set of secret messages contained within the texts. However, what they discovered within the first parchment was a highly unclear sort of communication.

The first parchment's coded message read:

Pastora there is no temptation that Poussin Teniers they keep the key peace 681 by the cross and this horse of God I finish that demon as guardian at midday blue apples.

The second parchment read:

To Dagobert II king and to Sion pertains this treasure and he is there dead.

Father Saunière went to see his superior, the Bishop of Carcassone, taking the parchments with him. The bishop then sent him on to the Parisian ecclesiastical authorities, so that he could show them these unusual documents. In Paris, Saunière met Abbott Bieil (the director general of the Saint-Sulpice seminary) and his nephew, Emil Hoffet. The latter had been preparing himself for the priesthood, yet he was also immersed in esotericism and was linked to groups, sects and secret societies, among which was the Priory of Sion. During his three-week stay in Paris, Saunière would also come into contact with these groups. On his return to Rennes-le-Chateau, he continued with the restoration of the church and made yet another find: he exhumed a tombstone dating from the 7th or 8th century and, below it, he also found a mortuary tomb containing skeletons. From that moment on, Saunière's financial status began to rise in such a manner that he was able to build a tower for his church – the Magdala Tower – he constructed an opulent country home for himself – Villa Bethania – that he never inhabited, he collected precious fabrics and ancient marbles, he built a zoo, he was visited by the Hapsburg Archduke on various occasions (among other illustrious guests), he treated his parishioners repeatedly to magnificent banquets fit for a king and decorated the church in a rather eccentric manner. For example, above the church porch he engraved the following inscription: *'Terribilis est locus iste'* ('this place is terrible'). Within the temple and underneath the baptismal font, the Abbott Saunière placed a statue of Asmodeus, the demonic guardian of hidden treasures and – according to an ancient Judaic legend – the builder of Solomon's Temple. In addition, he decorated the church with images belonging to the Stations of the Cross, yet they all seemed to contain some anomalous detail deviating from the Holy Scriptures. The whole of the temple's decoration appeared to form a sort of coded message sent by Saunière, but what exactly was this message? Finally, in 1917, after having been removed from office and subsequently reinstated to his post by the Vatican, Saunière passed away. Before that happened though, he was denied extreme unction by one of his colleagues, who had been called to his deathbed and had listened to his last confession.

His body was buried within the Magdala Tower, wrapped in a brightly coloured cassock adorned with scarlet tassels. Many of those who went to see his body would tear the tassels off his robe and take these away with them; a sort of ritual which nobody could ever explain.

So, where did Saunière's wealth come from? What did the concealed treasure the demon Asmodeus was guarding over consist of? Many researchers have suggested that the priest had uncovered some sort of treasure. If this was so, what was it? The hypotheses concerning the priest's secret treasure are numerous and varied: the history of the Rennes village and its environs could lead one to believe that there are numerous caches of precious jewels within the region; mostly because Rennes was the capital of the Northern Visigothic Empire. It was also the area in which the Cathars had settled, a group that was believed to be in possession of a fabulous treasure (the Holy Grail perhaps). Equally, it is possible that the Merovingian King Dagobert II hid the fruits of his conquests at this same village, which would additionally explain why the monarch is mentioned in

Mary Magdalene, Jesus' child, and the Holy Grail.

of the Rennes church parchments. Moreover, there has also been talk of a Templar treasure, which would in its turn explain the allusion to 'Sion' appearing in another one of the parchments. In addition, there has been a further hypothesis stating that perhaps Saunière had recovered the legendary treasure of the Temple of Jerusalem, and this is why the parchments allude to Sion. Nevertheless, beyond the possibility of Saunière having discovered – and made use of – a literal and material treasure, many researchers firmly believe that, in reality, the Abbot's true treasure was of a different nature altogether: it was a treasure that included an explosive secret capable in itself of changing the course of history; a secret of transcendental importance. Precious jewels, gold and money are not sufficient explanations to a whole series of questions, such as: why did Saunière get involved in occultist and Hermetic circles during his stay in Paris? Why did the Hapsburg Archduke visit such an unknown individual living in a small and recondite village in the Pyrenees? Why did Saunière engrave above the church threshold the words 'this place is terrible'? Why did the Vatican first remove him from his job, only to reinstate him later on? Why did the priest who was with Saunière at his deathbed refuse to give him the extreme unction after having listened to the dying man's last confession? What was it that Saunière confessed to? Could it have been linked to the human remains discovered within the chapel? A strictly material treasure would not explain the halo of mystery that surrounded – and still does – everything that is linked to Rennes-le-Chateau. So the question that arises is: what did the Rennes treasure consist of? The material treasure found – whether it actually existed or not – could in reality be a metaphor for another treasure: the remains of the Son of God himself. As is evidenced by the title of this section, Rennes-le-Chateau remains a mystery to this date. Although this has never been confirmed, an Anglican cleric, Alfred Leslie Lilley, has maintained that there exists irrefutable proof that the Crucifixion was a hoax, that Jesus Christ was still alive in 45 AD, and that he was buried in France; the proof to all of this (the nature of which is unknown) is to be found at the mysterious village church of Rennes-le-Chateau. If this sort of proof existed, and had indeed fallen into the hands of Abbott Saunière, his wealth could have been the payment made by the Vatican so that he would keep his knowledge a secret. As we shall see in the following chapter, secrets are not something foreign to the Holy See, quite the opposite.

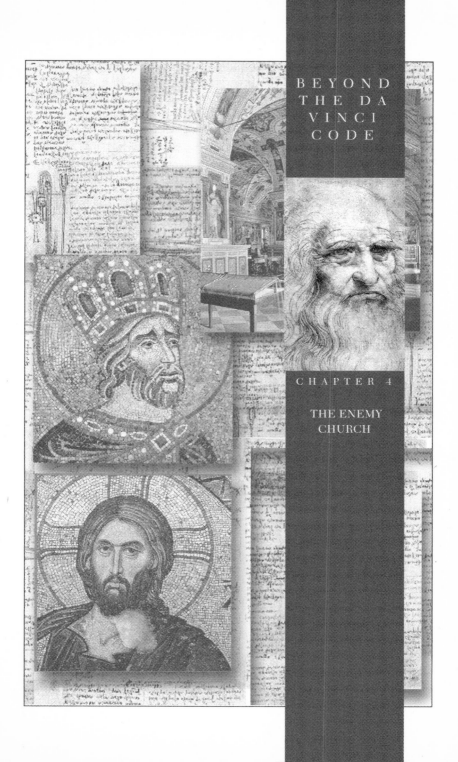

CHAPTER 4

THE ENEMY
CHURCH

THE ENEMY CHURCH

Are the Apocrypha the only texts to have been silenced by the Church? Is the existence of a line of direct descendants of Jesus Christ the sole secret guarded by this institution? If this closely guarded secret were to be made public, it would undoubtedly diminish the power of the Catholic Church enormously... The answer to both of these questions is negative. The Vatican has always been home to numerous secrets, intrigues, conspiracies, and mysteries...and just the same as the secret services of any state, it has used its power and influence (and still does) on numerous occasions of which common citizens are unaware.

Among the enormous range of secrets that are kept by the Church, the following chapter shall only concern itself with two issues. We will delve into the available information regarding the Vatican's secret archives, as these are linked to the secret concerning Jesus Christ and his descendants. We will also study the most talked about scandal of the last few decades involving the Holy See: the supposed murder of Pope John Paul I. Surrounded by gossip concerning the Mafia, Freemasonry, and financial scandals, it has been rumoured by some that this supposed murder could have been committed by people working for the Vatican.

THE VATICAN'S SECRET ARCHIVES

Fifty kilometres of subterranean shelves: books, codices and a multitude of parchments, all inaccessible to the general public; written records stored for two millennia, and which nobody knows for certain what they consist of. So why is this confidential and mysterious documentation kept at the Vatican? What arcane secrets do the Vatican's archives hold? It is impossible to recount in its entirety what is stored at this gigantic library; the majority of what is kept there remains unknown to those who are unable to access its venerable and enigmatic corridors. In spite of this, what follows is a brief listing of the texts that have been confirmed to reside within the secret archives of the Holy See:

• Documentation on primitive Christianity, including research studies on the Dead Sea scrolls.
• The Trial of the Knights Templar. A volume dating from 1309 concerning the trial of the knights of the Order of the Temple (see: chapter 2). This is a copy, not the original edition, yet it is thought to be an absolutely accurate version produced immediately after the original.

• The Western Schism (1378-1417), including the years in which there were three Popes in existence at the same time. Each one of them was surrounded by his own mysteries, secrets, and textual archives containing confidential documents.

• The Papal bull of Innocent VII (1484), a document in which the Holy Father instigated witch hunting.

• All of the books banned by the Vatican through its Collection Index; books that have, logically, been read in order to be archived. The Index holds its origins in the establishment of the Holy Congregation of the Holy Office (1542), a document officially implementing the Inquisition with a similar structure to the organization already existing in Spain. We must however clarify that the practice of prohibiting the printing, copying and reading of certain works had already began at the Council of Nicaea (see: chapter 1) where – for example – *Thaleia*, by early Greek Christian theologian Arius, was interdicted and burned.

• All of the existing information regarding the Roman calendar reform (which led to the calendar in use today) advanced by Pope Gregory XIII in the year 1582.

• A large quantity of material covering 'normal' subject matters (such as ecclesiastical, civil, and political topics), as well as – without a doubt – an equally large body of intelligence on paranormal affairs. Many researchers (Huc de Sant Joan de Mata among them) agree in that the Vatican's Secret Archives contain a large amount of evidence regarding paranormal phenomena and, in particular, parapsychology. Logically, an occurrence of this kind recorded during the 10th century would not have been labelled as a 'parapsychological phenomenon', but as an anathema, or perhaps as a miracle. During the centuries that followed, this same happening would have been linked to witchcraft.

• A complete set of documentation concerning Giordano Bruno, a Dominican brother from Italy who was brought to trial in the 16th century accused of heterodoxy; his trial lasted seven years. The only summary proceedings in existence are a set of fifty-five pages discovered in 1940.

• Within the archive section labelled as 'Archive of Miscellanious Works', we can find the complete trial proceedings of Cristina de Rovales, which took place during the 16th century. Sister Cristina was a nun belonging to the Third Order of Saint Dominic. She was taken to court regarding demonic possession, stigma, ghostly apparitions and other phenomena that would today be considered as purely parapsychological occurrences, such as levitation and telepathy.

• Texts from non-Christian countries that had been visited by missionaries. For example, during the 17th century, the Jesuits were working as

THE VATICAN EXPOSES ITS SECRET ARCHIVES

On 15 February, the Vatican announced that it will partially open its secret archives. The documents that will be made available for inspection will be those prior to the Second World War. Access to these documents will be granted only to researchers who make an official petition. The archives open to them will be those covering the period between the years 1922 and 1939. In this way, the Catholic Church intends to clear the name of Pope Pius XII, accused by Judaic organizations of having done very little to denounce the Holocaust. During the years prior to World War II, the man who would later on become Pope Pius XII was employed as ambassador for the Vatican in the city of Berlin.

DESTROYED DOCUMENTS

The initial six hundred and forty documents that will be made available next year to scholars cover the relations between the Holy See and Germany from 1922 to 1939. The Vatican however has made a public announcement stating that many of the paper files dating from the period between 1931 and 1934 were 'practically destroyed or dispersed' during the Allied bombings on Berlin, as well as by a fire (all of this reported by the Reuters news agency). In the meantime, the documents covering the period between 1939 and 1949 dealing with World War II prisoners of war will be made available on a later occasion. The textual material containing information regarding the existing relations between Pope Pius XII and Germany (up until the Pope's death in 1958) will be made available to scholars and researchers within a period of three years.

A PARTIAL OPENING

The Vatican has always defended the position maintained by Pope Pius XII, stating that his silence was due to the fear of endangering even further the lives of both Catholics and Jews. In a press release from early 2002, the Holy See declared that it hoped that the documents that have been made accessible will prove 'the enormous amount of charity and assistance work undertaken by Pope Pius XII, and how he aided the prisoners and victims of war, making no nationality, religion, or race distinctions.'

The above announcement was made some time after both Jewish and Catholic scholars that had been examining the Vatican's archives adjourned their activities, due to the fact that the Vatican was unwilling to make available its complete archived documentation. The Holy See agreed with these scholars that the partial exposition of the archives must be truly frustrating for them. Nevertheless, it explained that this was due to the necessity of protecting the Holocaust victims who were still alive.

BBBWORLD.com, 28 December 2002.

The Vatican's Library is open to the general public, yet it also possesses a subterranean secret archive that is only accessible to a privileged few.

missionaries in China, and sent back to Europe a truly astounding amount of textual material.

• Documentation about Galileo Galilei's trial in the 17th century.

• Letters sent by Pope Pius XII that reveal information regarding the relationship between the Vatican and Hitler.

The Vatican's secret archives were open to investigation and research for the first time, and only in part, in 1881. Since then, many of the books and documents that they contain have been published and analysed. Within the last few years, researchers have started the process of microfilming, video recording, and – of course – electronically archiving all of the available material through the use of computers.

THE CASE OF JOHN PAUL I

On 29 September 1978, the Vatican released an official announcement stating that the Holy Father, John Paul I, had passed away after having occupied his post for little more than thirty days. According to the Holy See's initial account of events, about half past five in the morning, the Pope's personal secretary found him dead in his bed with the lights switched on. Dr R. Buzonetti was immediately called to the Pope's deathbed, and after examining the body, he stated that the death had probably taken place around eleven o'clock on the previous night, caused by an acute heart attack. This was the first account of events released by the Vatican, yet later on it would become publicly known that these events had taken place differently; so differently in fact, that even to this date the death of Pope John Paul I continues to be an unsolved mystery.

The Vatican's second version of events was released shortly after the first one. Pieces of evidence that had been put together subsequently confirmed that it had not been the Pope's personal secretary who had found him dead, but a nun, Sister Vincenza. She discovered the Pontiff's dead body when, after having repeatedly knocked on his door and received no reply, she entered his room. When she walked in, she found him dead in his office, sitting at his desk, with a secret document pertaining to the Secretariat of State lying open on top of the table. Sister Vincenza quickly ran to wake the Pope's secretary, who confirmed the Pontiff's death and called in Cardinal Villot. The Cardinal examined the body together with a doctor and, soon after, they wasted no time in calling for the embalmers. An additional stumbling block: the statements made by the investigators of the Pope's death did not coincide with those of the other witnesses. The prelate's body was still warm when the embalmers arrived (a fact that was additionally verified by Sister Vincenza) and, therefore, the embalmers estimated that the death must have taken place between four and five in the morning of that same day, not around eleven o'clock on the previous night, as Dr R. Buzonetti had initially declared. At first, Sister Vincenza was forced to swear to an oath of silence by the Secretariat of State, yet in the end the brave Sister broke her unwillingly made oath, as she believed that the world should know the truth regarding the death of John Paul I, a man whom she deeply admired.

Almost immediately after the death, and in spite of receiving heated protests from several ecclesiastic officials, Cardinal Oddi declared that the Sacred College of Cardinals was not prepared to consider the possibility of initiating an investigation regarding the Pope's death. Equally, it would not accept any inspections, or any type of control exerted by any other outside person or entity. No medical bulletin was published and the Holy See did not allow a post mortem to be performed on the Pope. Because of these circumstances, and – most importantly – because of the numerous questions that were being raised by an increasingly intrigued general public, some cardinals asked to be made aware of the precise circumstances in which the death of John Paul I had taken place. Yet the contradictory accounts of events and stumbling blocks continued. Without performing a post mortem, it was clinically impossible to find out if the death had been caused by an acute heart attack, as had originally been stated. The Pope's lifestyle had been a sober one and his blood pressure had generally been low, which made the probability of a heart attack difficult, if not impossible.

To top it all off, the medical doctor who signed the Pope's death certificate confessed that he had never previously lent his services to the prelate, and was therefore unaware of his general state of health. Doctor da Ros, the Pope's personal physician, assured that he had seen him on the previous day, and that he had found him to be in a good state of health.

As time passed, the doubts increased and multiplied. One of the specialists in charge of investigating the circumstances surrounding the

---

THE DEATH OF JOHN PAUL I

An event of the enormous proportions and enigmatic circumstances that we have just described could not – of course – have passed unnoticed by literature, including fiction, essays, and investigative works. All of the works produced on the subject of the mysterious death of Pope John Paul I have been documented in varying degrees; some have based their accounts on fiction, while others have based themselves on fact. A whole series of titles, as well as a large number of journalistic articles (including the enormous amount of articles appearing in newspapers all over the world) approached the Pope's mysterious and yet to be resolved death in different ways. Some of these texts are the following:

• *The Pope has been Murdered (Operation Dove)*, written by journalists Jesús Ramón Peña and Mario Edoardo Zottola, maintains the theory that the death of John Paul I was the result of purely financial reasons. The Vatican's financial empire is one of the most powerful in the world and, because this, there existed important motives to eliminate the leading overseer of this gigantic fortune.

• *A Murderer for John Paul I?* Written by fiction writer Bruce Marshall, this novel consists of a plot whereby Pope Luciani is poisoned by a fictitious society named 'The New Apostles'. The members of this society are opposed to the changes imposed by the second Vatican Council, and support Cardinal Siri – instead of Cardinal Luciani – as the new Pontiff.

Pope's death (Dr Cabrera) suggested the possibility that it could have been the result of depressant substances, which could be lethal in certain doses to someone who suffered from low blood pressure. Cardinal Villot's particular and suspicious hurry to embalm the Pope's body now also became more noticeable. Some versions said that the embalming was performed without extracting any of the Pontiff's blood or organs, while other versions stated that the embalmers removed parts of the Pope's body, possibly his internal organs.

A quarter of a century later, it is obvious that none of the above circumstances have been explained, and the death of John Paul I remains to date an unresolved mystery. Nevertheless, the facts revealed seem to point in a single direction: a series of murky manoeuvres linked to the Vatican of which the Pope had been aware. So who was involved in these manoeuvres? The Vatican Bank and Propaganda 2 'Masonic' Lodge (P2).

• Certain journals and magazines belonging to extreme right groups accused Archbishop Marcinkus (banker for the Vatican), Cardinal Villot (Secretary of State for the Holy See), and a number of other prelates of forming part of a Masonic society. For this reason, Roman Traditionalists, followers of Archbishop Lefevre, looked into the possibility of Pope Luciani having been murdered by Masons that had infiltrated the highest spheres of the Vatican.

• *The Red Cassock.* Written by Roger Peyrefitte, this work of fiction describes Pope Luciani as a keen reformer intent on eradicating the corruption existing within the ecclesiastical cupola. The Pope's reforms trigger a conspiracy devised by certain prelates, who maintained close relations with financiers, Mafiosi, and leaders of the P2 Lodge. In this book, Villot and Marcinkus are portrayed as the instigators of the Pope's murder, which is performed by a hitman with the use of a poisoned syringe.

• *The Truth About the Death of John Paul I,* written by Jean Jacques Thierry, presents an extreme hypothesis: it suggests that Cardinal Villot supplanted Pope Paul VI with a double, and that he also planned the death of his successor when Pope Luciani discovered the infiltration of Masons within the Holy See. According to Thierry, the murder of Pope Luciani took place when he discovered the relations existing between the Church and the Mafia.

(continued on next page)

P2, THE VATICAN BANK, AND THE MURDER
OF JOHN PAUL I?

In order to unravel this complicated web of power and corruption, we must first begin with a brief explanation regarding those who managed the intrigue: Michele Sindona, Licio Gelli, and Paul Marcinkus.

Sindona began his career by recycling the fortune of the Gambino clan, a well known North American gangster family. This was to be the initial point in the forging of an international financial empire. Later on, and through the mediations of he who would in time become Pope Paul VI, Sindona met Massimo Spada, the managing director of the Vatican Bank. This allowed the Italo-American Mafia to utilize the Vatican's financial

---

THE DEATH OF JOHN PAUL I (continues)

• *In God's Name: an Investigation into the Murder of Pope John Paul I* by David A. Yallop. This book is the result of three years of investigative research. Some members of the Church secretly collaborated with Yallop in his investigation. He maintains that the Vatican concealed the circumstances surrounding the Pope's death, and that it is therefore necessary to open an official investigation. Yallop's book provoked a true commotion, to the point of driving Jean Parvulesco to accept the possibility of the Pope having been executed to prevent him from leading the Church into a progressive path in aid of the Third World. The Papal Commission for Social Communications also reacted to this book, driven to publicly state that an atmosphere of intrigue and conspiracies was something alien to the Vatican, and that the Pope's health was altogether weak.

• *Pontiff,* written by G. Thomas and M. Morgan-Witts, suggests that the Pope's murder was in fact a rumour, skilfully spread by the KGB so as to discredit the Vatican. This was due to the fact that, at that moment in time, political relations between the USSR and the Holy See were going through a very tense phase.

• In his book *You Will Be Held to Account: the Death and Character of Pope John Paul I,* the priest and author Father Jesús López Sáez sustains the thesis that the prelate was murdered and declares himself to be in favour of an investigation.

institutions in order to launder dirty money originating from various criminal activities, many of them mafia-related.

Sindona then struck a friendship with Licio Gelli, Grand Master of P2 and a powerful textile impresario, whose curriculum vitae included among other dubious honours, that of belonged at one time to the SS.

Once they became friends, Gelli and Sindona gained access to the highest spheres of the Vatican accompanied by Umberto Ortolani, a lawyer and gentleman-in-waiting to His Holiness (and who would subsequently become Gelli's lieutenant within the P2). It is at this point in time that the third protagonist of the story makes his appearance, Paul Marcinkus. He

• *A Thief in the Night: Life and Death in the Vatican*, by journalist John Cornwell, is the result of an investigation instigated by the Vatican; because of this, they offered Cornwell unprecedented access to information. This allowed the author – among other things – to interview the protagonists of the story who were still alive. This book is a far cry from the conspiracy theories that we have been presenting up until now. *A Thief in the Night* states the following in relation to the Pope: 'his meekness, his distrust, his constant worrying regarding purely pastoral and pious issues did not adapt well to a Church that had to confront the worldly challenges of the eighties and nineties.' In an even harsher manner, Cornwell pronounces that 'the clues began to lead me to a conclusion that seems to be more shameful than any of the conspiracy theories proposed up until now. They despised him for his clumsy manner of walking, for how he appeared to have lost interest, for his naive speeches and his simple language, and they also made fun of his whistling tone of voice. They referred to him in a condescending tone, using short versions of his name. There were constant stories running around regarding his behaviour and how he would say or do the wrong thing. (...) He allowed himself to die because he did not feel capable of being the Pope. He died alone, in the centre of the largest Christian community in the world, due to negligence and lack of love, ridiculed and scorned by the same institution that existed to sustain him.'

• In *The Secret Journal of John Paul I*, its author – Ricardo de la Cierva – purports that Pope Luciani died due to strictly natural causes, although he admits that there did exist a series of circumstances surrounding his death that were linked to some sort of conspiracy (death threats, a corrupt financial plot, etc.).

John Paul I

was an archbishop who held the full trust of Pope Paul VI, as he had been his bodyguard and had once saved his life. When Marcinkus was put in charge with managing the Institute for Religious Works (IOR), the Vatican's financial apparatus, he used Sindona's banking web in order to invest part of the fortune of the Holy See. At the same time and in a parallel manner, Sindona was making use of the institutional structure of the Vatican in order to launder Mafia money and evade taxes. On the other hand, and creating a sort of 'perfect structure', Gelli was using the enormous power of P2 to guarantee political cover for their operations. So where was this apparently perfectly organized financial structure heading?

By 1973, Sindona was the most important banker in Italy. Among other individuals of high standing and power who dedicated their eulogies to him, the Italian Prime Minister and the US ambassador publicly praised him. However, a lethal combination that included – among other elements – the petroleum crisis and a series of speculative operations, contributed to the end of the banker's empire. When his financial downfall took place, Sindona fled to the United States, while the Vatican lost a sizeable amount of its money. The latter fact was strongly denied by Marcinkus, who would later on even claim that he did not know Sindona.

While he was employed as the assistant director general of Banco Ambrosiano, Roberto Calvi – who knew Paul VI as an archbishop in Milan – got in touch with Sindona, probably through the intervention of Marcinkus and Spada. What were the reasons behind this meeting? The

IOR was the proprietor of a good part of the shares of Banco Ambrosiano and of practically half of Finabank (one of the Swiss banks used by Sindona to disguise his financial machinations). With the IOR as financial back-up, Calvi became the president of Banco Ambrosiano in the early 1970s. Shortly after, he was also employed as the treasurer of P2. After Sindona's fall, the IOR asked Calvi to manage its overseas investments, and even lent him its name so that Calvi could buy half of the shares of the Banca Mercantile in Florence.

In 1977, after having been arrested in New York and accused of fraud, Sindona reminded Calvi that half of his businesses belonged to him (Sindona). Despite this reminder, Calvi did not keep his promise of sending Sindona money, and so the latter went on to fill Milan with posters denouncing Calvi as a fraudster, a swindler and a money launderer. As a last resort, he even sent a letter to the governor of the Bank of Italy, the content of which finally trapped Calvi in a definitive manner.

PAUL MARCINKUS, BISHOP AND BANKER

Paul Marcinkus was a judo expert, a drinker of quality whisky and an excellent golf player. He was also the first bishop to be a member of the administration council of the Bank of Nassau, a famous fiscal paradise where many of Roberto Calvi's illegal operations had taken place. Marcinkus was accused of being involved in the bankruptcy of the Banco Ambrosiano, and it was also rumoured that he had intervened in the suspicious death of John Paul I and in the 'suicide' of Roberto Calvi, who was found hanging from Blackfriars Bridge in London. But both the Supreme and the Constitutional tribunals stopped the judges in Milan from taking Marcinkus to trial for his implication in the bankruptcy of Banco Ambrosiano. The arrest orders failed when the bishop took refuge within Vatican City. No cardinal from the Papal Curia dared stand against him, most probably because he had helped all of them financially. On the contrary, Pope John Paul II remained a staunch defender of Marcinkus for the duration of the whole scandal, possibly because it was the bishop banker who had financed the Polish Solidarity Movement. So, what was the conclusion to this story? The Vatican agreed to pay two hundred and fifty million dollars to the Italian State after the bankruptcy of Banco Ambrosiano took place – a bank of which the Vatican was a shareholder – stating that it was doing this freely, as a personal token of financial assistance.

It is within this highly complex panorama that John Paul I makes his first appearance; in August of 1978, Paul VI died, and the cardinals elected Albino Luciani as his successor – Pope John Paul I. John Paul I was a very different Pontiff to his predecessors, though, and brought with him a decided air of reform. Furthermore, he had already proved to have a firm character during the famous financial scandal that took place in 1972: the sale to Calvi of the Catholic Bank of Veneto, a financial operation masterminded by Marcinkus. On this particular occasion, Luciani was asked by the bishops to initiate an investigation and he found out, among other things, that the bank in question had been transformed after the sale. From being an entity that favoured people with low incomes by offering low interest credit loans, it had been turned into a financial society merely dedicated to evading taxes and to illegal speculation.

When he became Pope, John Paul was already well aware of what to expect in this regard. He put Cardinal Villot in charge of the financial inspection of the IOR. In the meantime, Calvi started selling his shares, and this is when he found out that the new pontiff had decided to find a substitute for Marcinkus, as well as to return the Church to its position of Evangelical poverty and bar Masons from the priesthood. In order to protect his own interests Calvi ensured that, on 12 September, John Paul I had received a list containing the names of one hundred and twenty-one Vatican employees who were presumably Masons; specifically, those belonging to P2, and who would therefore be forced to leave their employment immediately. Of course, on this list were Villot and Marcinkus, who were at the time the secretary of the Vatican State and the executive director of the Vatican Bank respectively.

The Pope had in his way started a revolution that was secretly applauded by the majority of the clergy and had the potential to become truly devastating for the minority of the clergy who held most of the power. Through his revolution, John Paul I planned to transform the Church and to give it renewed purpose, with the result that many of the individuals who had been holding on to power would be dispossessed of it – by force.

According to several testimonies, Pope Luciani meant to replace Cardinal Villot with Cardinal Benelli – Marcinkus' greatest adversary – and, on the evening of the 28th, he held a long conversation with Villot to inform him of his decision. Just hours later, the Pope was deady.

BEYOND
THE DA
VINCI
CODE

CHAPTER 5

OPUS DEI

OPUS DEI

'He was broad and tall, with ghost-pale skin and thinning white hair. His irises were pink with dark red pupils.' This is the description that Dan Brown makes of Silas, the fanatic assassin of *The Da Vinci Code*. Silas is, first and foremost, a member of Opus Dei; this fact forms a fundamental part of his identity. Yet... what exactly is the institution of Opus Dei? Throughout the years it has been portrayed as a Catholic and ultraconservative destructive cult, and as a religious Mafia organization. Many of those who once formed part of its ranks and subsequently abandoned the group tell the most terrible stories.

In order to understand this organization properly it is necessary to begin by telling the story of its founder. We will then go on to explain the way in which it is organized. We will also examine the initiation rituals that form part of its admissions process, and we will look at its formative and instruction methods, including its code of conduct; a code that must be followed daily and strictly by all of its members. We shall study all of these issues within the present chapter.

A BRIEF HISTORY OF 'THE WORK OF GOD'

The Vatican's personal prelature generally known as Opus Dei (The Work of God) was founded in the year 1928 by the Spanish priest Josemaría Escrivá de Balaguer y Alvás. Escrivá was born on 9 January 1902 in the Spanish province of Huesca. He was the son of a merchant dealer, although the official history of Opus Dei states that Escrivá belonged to an aristocratic family.

Opus Dei originated within the small nucleus formed by Escrivá and his family, at what he termed the 'student residence', which was in reality a family home where Escrivá would invite and receive his followers.

After being founded, and with Franco's dictatorship holding power over Spain for decades, the philosophy and practices of Opus Dei became totally necessary to the existing authoritarian clergy organization. It is at this time that Opus Dei began proselytising, basically through its infiltration within different university groups, as well as within several executive groups within the business sector. On an economic level, the Spanish Banco Popular (Popular Bank) can be considered Opus Dei's first major financial work of a high order. Through its formation, Opus Dei members now possessed their own independent financial backing. To make things even better for the group, Pope John Paul II canonized Escrivá on 6 October

2002 (he had already beatified him in 1992). In his canonization speech, the Pope proclaimed the following:

...Saint Josemaría was chosen by the Lord to give voice to a universal call to sanctity and to point out that everyday life, common activities, constitute the path to sanctification. It could be said that he was the saint of the ordinary.

At the same time, Opus Dei decided to go beyond the boundaries of its country of origin. Using its native Spain as its base, and through years of hard work, Opus Dei has never stopped its international expansion. This international propagation has essentially been carried out by its Spanish numerary members, who were the first to go out into the world in order to spread the sanctifying message of the organization. Opus Dei's first ambassadors were Fernando Maicas (in France), Luís María Garrido (in the United States), and Ramón Montalat (in Brazil). Eventually, the Work of God also expanded into the United Kingdom, Italy, Portugal and Mexico. From the 1950s onwards, its expansion continued into Venezuela, Canada, Argentina, Germany, Holland, Switzerland and other countries, both European and American. Finally, its evangelizing mission was extended onto further continents, including countries such as Japan, Kenya, North Africa, Australia, Nigeria, the Philippines, etc.

At present, there are more than eighty thousand members of Opus Dei spread across more than sixty countries. In addition, and as it is explained in *The Da Vinci Code*, this religious organization possesses a central headquarters in New York which is valued at over forty-seven million dollars.

THE STRUCTURE OF OPUS DEI

Let us now look at the internal organization and structure of The Work of God:

• Opus Dei's bureaucratic apparatus is – at a first glance – a sort of imitation of the bureaucracy of the Roman Catholic Church. At an international level, it has a President and a General Council, both based in Rome, next to Vatican City. A secretary, a solicitor, a group of four advisors, a prefect of studies and an administrator form the General Council.
• At a national level, regional councils form the highest executive offices. Contact between the General Council in Rome and the international regional councils is brought about through the so-called 'missus': he is

considered to be a messenger from the Father serving as a link between the two councils. The Papal 'nuncio' performs a similar task within the bureaucracy of the Vatican.
• In its links with the Vatican, Opus Dei also has the help of a Protector Cardinal working within the Holy See. This is a nominal post, and serves as an official intermediary between the organization and the diverse departments of the Vatican.
• Within the hierarchy of the order, and below the regional councils, we find the local councils, which exist in all of the cities where the organization has managed to establish itself.
• Within Opus Dei residential centres, there exists a directorship, which is always filled by a priest, who is helped by an assistant director, a role that is generally occupied by a dynamic youth, followed by a secretary. The director is in charge of the spiritual activities of the residents and the neophytes, while the assistant director is in charge of all practical and logistical activities supporting the functioning of the residence centre. The centre is organised in dedication to the patrons of The Work of God. There exists therefore a 'Saint Gabriel manager' in charge of domestic tasks, a

---

THE OPUS DEI 'FAMILY'

Like all other sectarian organizations, Opus Dei possesses its own particular jargon that is only known by its members. This 'internal language' operates as a sort of 'filter' for external reality, transforming the latter into something useful for the internal life of Opus Dei resident members. Speaking differently to the rest of the population, with the use of exclusive codes, and in a different way to that in which people in the 'outside' world speak, separates the neophyte from the outer world. Moreover, it generates in him or her a feeling of belonging that involves him more deeply with the rest of the group.

   In this regard, it is of particular interest the way in which a sort of 'family' is constructed in an organization through the use of specific terminology. Among the ranks that form the organization, the founder is known in internal jargon as 'the Father', the Work is 'the Mother' and all of the members of the brotherhood are its 'Children', addressing each other as 'Brothers'. Escrivá's mother is 'the Grandmother', and members talk about Escrivá's siblings as 'Aunt Carmen' and 'Uncle Santiago'. The term 'family life' refers to the type of existence and relationships that are developed through contact with other members of Opus Dei.

'Saint Raphael manager' in charge of new members, and a 'Saint Michael manager' who is in charge of the numeraries and other supporters of the organization. These posts are generally filled on a rota basis and are designated by the assistant director.

THE STRUCTURE'S HIERARCHY

What sorts of people are able to become members of this organization, and in what way do they join its ranks? Opus Dei is governed by a rigid social structure, with a series of levels that are very similar to the Indian system of castes, and which are based on a series of different criteria such as physical availability, social class, physical beauty and state of health.

• **Numerary**: within this category we find single individuals of both sexes, who are blessed with an excellent physical presence and possess graduate degrees. The latter requisite is not indispensable and can be replaced by a considerable amount of money, a good web of social contacts or by exceptional personal qualities. Numerary members form a sort of elite within the organization and they live in Opus Dei residential centres.

• **Associate**: this group is also formed by single individuals of either sex, yet they do not hold graduate studies, or do possess graduate studies but have a physical defect or chronic illness, or have a family member/s dependent on their employment.

• **Supernumerary**: this level within the organization includes married individuals of either sex, or those who, without being married, are considered to be 'not good enough' by the organization. They are viewed as the support troops of the organization and, in fact, they constitute the brotherhood's best breeding ground as they are obliged to bring to the world 'all of the children sent by God', and to educate them at Opus Dei schools.

• **Co-operator**: this is the lowest level in the organization, and its members are not even obliged to follow the Catholic faith. They are not considered to be true Opus Dei members (this is why they are called 'co-operators'), and they are solely expected to help The Work of God economically, and to take part once in a while in its 'seclusion courses'.

The media throughout the Western world reported the canonization of Josemaría Escrivá.

RECRUITMENT TECHNIQUES

But... how, and in what way, does Opus Dei recruit its members? Before we start to list the different ways in which Opus Dei recruitment techniques take place, it is most important that we point out the following: Escrivá's work, *The Way*, states quite clearly that Opus Dei does not welcome the masses into its ranks, but that it employs a selective recruitment policy. Escrivá's aims are to attract the wise, the powerful and the virtuous into his organization. In his *Constitutions of the Sacerdotal Society of the Holy Cross and Opus Dei* we may read the following:

To work with all of our might so that the social class known as 'the intellectual' – which serves as a guide to civil society due to its teachings, which have no equal, as well as due to the roles that it performs and the social prestige by which it distinguishes itself – embraces the precepts of Our Lord Jesus Christ and puts them into practice.

In this respect, Opus Dei is indistinguishable from any other sect, most of which generally search for recruits among the most capable, active, and educated individuals in society.

Nevertheless, although from its early days (and even today) the organization has mainly directed itself to professionals and university graduates, it also addresses a more humble and less elitist public. It does

111

Josemaría Escrivá

this through the use of the 'breeding ground' of the Order, what they term the 'Task of Saint Raphael'.

To begin with, the organization approaches young people through institutions of education. Some of these constitute Corporate Works – that is, schools that depend entirely on Opus Dei – while others are solely guided by the spiritual directives recommended by The Work. Schoolteachers do not generally perform the organization's propaganda work; preceptors and students who are already Opus Dei members are usually employed in this role. Universities also hold a fundamental post in regards to recruitment, and their recruitment structure is very similar to that of schools. Furthermore, the recruitment of young people may take place, in fact, within any educational institution or youth club in which they assemble. Once the organization considers that a young person is ready to be recruited, he or she is invited into the so-called Circle of Saint Raphael. Once within this circle, meetings of fewer than ten people take place, where the Circle's director explains a series of Christian doctrinal issues from the specific viewpoint of the organization. Later on, the director of the Circle speaks in private and individually with each one of the novice recruits. In this way, and with the use of persuasive techniques that do not exclude emotional blackmail (see: Brainwashing), the young person is led towards the ranks of Opus Dei.

Yet the organization does not limit its recruitment tactics to educational and pedagogic circles. Within the hospitals where Opus Dei holds some influence, the gratitude of the patients who have been cured is used to introduce them into the philosophy of Opus Dei.

INITIATION RITUALS

In order to become a full member of Opus Dei, an individual must start by writing a letter accompanied by four passport-sized photographs of him- or herself. Within his or her application, the claimant briefly reveals his aims, and asks to be allowed to become a membe of a specific rank within the organization: numerary, associate, supernumerary or co-operator. The latter is an extremely important aspect of the application, because of the organization's pyramidal power structure where hierarchy is of essential importance to its smooth functioning. It is worth mentioning that an Opus Dei priest must have previously recommended the specific rank solicited by the applicant. This priest is employed to direct the thoughts of the applicant during his or her preparation period (the period previous to the actual membership application).

This initial application step is known in Opus Dei jargon as 'whistling'. The applicant's letter, together with a report written by those responsible for the residential centre where the application has been entered, is sent to Rome, where Opus Dei's General Council, as well as its principal headquarters, are to be found.

During the following months (roughly six), what is known within the organization as 'performing the admission' takes place. This process implies that the candidate is legally and effectively linked to Opus Dei through an admission ceremony.

This admission ceremony consists of a simple ritual, whereby the petitioner reads out a concise declaration standing in front of an empty black cross (without a crucified Jesus Christ on it), with the director and priest of the residential centre acting as witnesses. The residential priest is also in charge of performing the ceremony. In addition to this formal declaration, the applicant has to swear to vows of poverty, chastity and obedience.

A year after this official admission, the 'offering' ritual takes place. At this point in time – a year and a half after the 'whistling' – it is presumed that the neophyte has been living according to the 'spirit of The Work', and that he or she is ready to begin his or her own proselytising tasks in an efficient manner.

After the 'offering' has been performed, and each year thereafter, the newcomer must renew the vows he or she made during the initial admission ceremony; this takes place every year on 19 March (Saint Joseph's Day). A mass is celebrated for the oath renewal and, after the consecration of the wafer and the chalice has been performed, the new member of Opus Dei is obliged to repeat his or her promise of devotion to The Work.

Six years after the 'offering' ceremony, the final ritual takes place. This is the ceremony of fidelity, and it constitutes an ultimate confirmation. From then on, it is not necessary for the new member to renew his or her vows yearly, on 19 March. Within this final ceremony, the neophyte receives a ring that he or she will have to wear for life, and which accredits him or her as an established and permanent Opus Dei member.

INDUCTION METHODS

It is obvious that in order to form and maintain such a clearly pyramidal, discriminatory and hierarchical structure, it is necessary to 'educate' and to convince those who intend to form a part of it that they are on the right path. Their conviction must be strong and run deep, so much so that its followers must be willing to punish their bodies daily with the use of the cilice (just as we mentioned elsewhere in the book). Yet, how does Opus Dei implant in its members this complete loyalty and profound belief in the mission of the organization?

The organization's most important indoctrination methods in order to achieve this are the following:

• **Classes and coexistence conventions**: these gatherings take place once a year and last thirty-five days for the numeraries, and fifteen days for the associates and the supernumeraries. Obviously, members must spend the duration of the course living according to the 'daily life conduct' rules of the organization. In addition, they must attend a series of classes and seminars on The Work, practise sports, meet daily with other members for an informal chat following each lunch and dinnertime and study catechism and theology.

• **Seclusion retreats**: these instructional gatherings were previously known as 'spiritual exercises', and also take place once a year. Their last six days for the numeraries and between three to five days for the associates and the supernumeraries. During seclusion retreats, the attendees have to follow strictly the daily life norms of the organization, as well as attend numerous meditation gatherings, talks on 'the spirit of The Work', and prayer meetings.

•**Brief gatherings**: these take place every one or two weeks. They begin with a short commentary on the Gospels, followed by a spiritual examination that consists of reviewing Opus Dei's twenty-five essential spirituality points: chastity, obedience, poverty, proselytising, evangelizing, mortification, etc. This examination is followed by a talk, which in its turn is followed by an informal chat (this takes place after either lunch or dinner, and its purpose is to relax the members for a while, and therefore to improve the 'family life' of the residential centre). This informal chat is followed by the '*preces*' (prayers in the Latinate language created by Escrivá exclusively for Opus Dei members) and the so-called '*enmedatio*' (a sort of self-critique ceremony, in which the member must kneel down on the floor, in front of all of the other members of the residential centre, and state out loud all of the personal faults of which he or she repents).

• **Brotherly corrections**: this consists of correcting another member when he or she does something inappropriate or in opposition to 'the spirit of The Work'. In order to perform a brotherly correction, the member must first seek advice from the director of the residence and, if he approves, then the correction can take place. Once the correction has been 'given', the director of the residential centre must be made aware that the correction has already occurred.

• **Confidences**: this is a confession of one's faults that is made to either the director or another member of the Council or to a select member of the house where small groups of veteran members of The Work reside. In addition to making public the faults of its members, Opus Dei also assumes that it has the responsibility to shape their character and to increase 'the spirit of The Work' within them.

• **Chats**: these take place every fifteen days in the company of a priest. They are normally held in a collective group.

In spite of how amiable and friendly the above sound, they in fact constitute a cover for different modalities of a more veiled and frightening indoctrination method: the 'brainwashing' technique.

DAILY LIFE NORMS AND SELF-PUNISHMENT PRACTICES

Members who reside within an Opus Dei centre must follow a series of very strict daily life norms; particularly during their first years within the order. These conduct rules form an integral part of what is termed as 'the spirit of The Work'. Some of these are the following:

• After waking up, the resident member must kiss the floor and devote all of the day's work to God.
• Not to spend more that half an hour in getting ready and dressed in the mornings. Although it is no longer explicitly recommended to shower or bathe using cold water, some members still follow this practice.
• After breakfast, the resident member must go through a brief examination, and then must visit His Holiness. Within the so-called 'residences of The Work of God', the day begins with the 'minor silence',

Escrivá's canonization drew thousands of Opus Dei followers to Vatican Square. October 2002.

which lasts for three hours. The object of this is to think about the subject-matter of the prayer that is going to take place later on.

• After the resident member has decided on the subject matter of his or her prayer, he has to devote half an hour to it.

• Towards the end of the day, a further and general examination takes place, whereby members are asked to make a balance of that day's activities (including both spiritual and financial activities). Subsequently, the 'major silence' begins, whereby resident members are not allowed to speak until the following morning.

• Before going to bed, resident members must cross themselves, then sprinkle their bed with holy water, and kneel down with arms spread out forming a cross to say the three Hail Maries.

• When resident members are on the street or in other public places, they must 'guard their sight' so that they are able to avoid possible temptations that could assail them via their eyes. For this same purpose, they carry a crucifix in their pocket; in this way, they can hold it tightly when temptation overcomes them and, through this act, avoid falling into it.

Yet although all of the above constitute very strict rules (and these are not the only ones in existence), the fact is that Opus Dei goes even further in order to control the lives of those who decide to form a part of their organization. What we are referring to are mortification or self-punishment practices that, although they are no longer compulsory as they once were, are still maintained to date. These are the following:

• To wear the cilice belt (a leather strap studded with sharp metal barbs) for two hours a day.
• To use the discipline (a heavy knotted rope that is slung over one's shoulder repeatedly) either on Saturday nights or on Sunday mornings.
• To sleep on top of a wooden board instead of a mattress.
• Once a week, on what is known as 'duty day', to sleep on the floor using a book instead of a pillow.

Other mortification practices that have been reported by those who once belonged to The Work are: to place stones in one's shoes, to abstain from drinking water and to force oneself to sleep for an insufficient number of hours.

THE WAY; A GUIDE FOR A PATH TO MORTIFICATION

The philosophy of Opus Dei is conservative, misogynous and elitist. It sets the bases for the spiritual and physical mortification of its members. Opus Dei ideology is clearly and explicitly explained in *The Way*, a compilation of almost one thousand maxims written by Escrivá and intended for meditation. Published in 1934, *The Way* went on to spread its message across the entire world. Escrivá's maxims recommend his followers not to be weak or soft, and to reject any type of self-compassion feelings. Among other arguments, Escrivá's work states the fact that Jesus Christ redeemed all of mankind through his sacrifice on the Cross, and so all good Christians must pursue the redemption of humanity by happily accepting to perform sacrifices. On this same order of things, the book considers the material body to be a vehicle for instincts and carnal passions, and so it must be defeated through the use of mortification of the flesh practices and acts of penance. Rigorous fasting is also highly recommended as an act of penance much approved of by God.

TESTIMONY

The Bitter Story of an Opus Dei Numerary, written by Agustina López de los Mozos Muñoz, was published in December 1988 by the prestigious French magazine *Marie Claire*. The following fragment will allow us to understand the way in which Opus Dei's organization functions; this is revealed through the brave words of one who experienced all of it in her own flesh:

One evening I walked into one of the numerary's rooms and, as there was only one chair, I sat down on the bed. I instantly felt a muffled knock. Had I made that noise? What had I just sat on? The numerary that was with me let out a giggle.

'Have you hurt yourself?'

'A little bit. But, what sort of a bed is this?'

'Well, you see, us numeraries sleep on top of a wooden board, without a mattress. The board is a specific height so that when it is covered with the bedspread, the bed has a normal appearance; just in case somebody who doesn't belong to The Work walks past.'

'And why do you sleep on top of a board?'

'The Father says that women need to control their bodies; that they must not allow their bodies to enjoy certain comforts as this will lead them into temptation.'

I lifted the bedspread and, to be sure, there was a wooden board covered by a blanket that also served as a mattress. On top of it she had placed the bed sheet.

The first time that I spent the night on top of a board, I didn't sleep at all. The only position it is possible to maintain when sleeping in these conditions is to lie on your back, you can't lie on your side as then all of your bones dig into you and it is completely impossible to sleep on your front. Nevertheless, after several months have passed, you manage to get used to it. I was still unaware though of another detail regarding the bed; well, not the bed, but rather the pillow. It was during one of the many talks that we had that they explained to us another one of The Work's customs: duty day. Once a week, each female numerary must feel spiritually responsible for the rest of the members of The Work, and in order to do this she would have to follow a special mortification practice, as well as having to pray for longer than usual. On duty night, the female numerary would have to use a telephone book as her pillow. The combination of wooden board and telephone book is a difficult experience to describe.

On another day, and also by chance, while I was with another numerary, in the office where she worked at the College Residence, I saw her bring out from a cabinet a metal box that seemed to contain chocolates or sweets. I asked her if I could have one, but she told me that the box was empty. Yet, when she moved it I thought it sounded as if there were something inside. And as I was quite friendly with her, I asked her what was inside the box. She replied with a teasing smile, and said that she should not be the one to tell me, because it should be my director who explained it to me, but that as the subject had come up... She opened the box and took out a rather strange belt; it was made out of plaited wire, with

spikes sticking out on the inner part of it.
She then took the belt by one of the two
bands that it had at each end, and lifted
it while she said: this is the cilice belt.
'I'm sorry, what did you say?'
'The cilice belt, girl. Have you never seen
one before?'
'I can promise you I haven't'
'Well, us female numeraries use it for two
hours every day.'
      At that moment I did not
understand how you could use the cilice
belt for two hours a day; I had already
met many female numeraries and had
not yet seen one wearing that strange
belt.

The cilice belt and the discipline rope.

'Look, you place the side of the belt with
the spikes on your thigh, up near your groin,
and with the strings at its ends you tie it on.
'I don't believe you!'
'I'm serious, truly, it's just another rule; two hours every day, excluding
Sundays and holidays.'
'But I'm sure you'll tie it on loosely, those spikes look sharp...'
'That depends on each one's individual generosity. The normal thing is that,
as it is a corporal mortification practice, and as we have to do it, we should
do it well. You should tie it on as tightly as you can. You wear it underneath
your skirt and nobody notices it.'
      I was handed the cilice belt and from then on I would wear it for
two hours every day. I would alternate the leg on which I wore it; one day
on one leg, on the next day on the other leg. When I would take it off, I
could feel how the spikes would tear away at the flesh, leaving my skin full
of small bleeding wounds – one wound for each spike. On the following day,
I would use the cilice on the other leg, and so I would leave a day in
between for the wounds to heal. But they were never able to heal
completely. The worst thing was when summer approached because the
College Residence had a swimming pool but my swimming costume was not
long enough to cover the wounds. And although we all used the cilice belt, it
was frowned upon to let others see the marks of your penance. This is also
the reason why female numeraries use bathing costumes with a little skirt,
like those used by pregnant women, or like the ones our grandmothers used
to wear. I can remember that, for a few weeks, I wore the cilice around my

waist instead of on my thigh. In this way, the marks were easier to cover up and the pain was not as strong. I imagine that I wasn't the only one that had though of this, because at one of our regular talks they made a special point of telling us that the cilice belt should be worn tied around the thigh, and that we should not invent other strange ways of wearing it. So I didn't repeat the waist experience again. We had to wear it when we were inside the house; that is, nobody should walk out into the street wearing it. The reason that we were given for this is that if I had an accident and was taken to hospital, it would be very shocking for people to see it. The problem with wearing it at the house was that, if you walked into someone in the corridor, you could be hit precisely on the spot where you were wearing your cilice. On those occasions, you would smile very forcibly and swear under your breath. To sit down when you are wearing your cilice belt is not a pleasant experience either. If you sat down and managed to find a reasonably comfortable position, you didn't want to get up again. And we had to do all of this without losing our smile, acting very naturally, which is a sign of having a very good spirit.

I found out about 'the discipline' after a year and a half of being a member of The Work. This is a corporal mortification practice: a whip made out of a strong rope with several strands. It is used on Saturdays, only on Saturdays. You walk into the bathroom, you take off your underwear and then, kneeling down on the floor, you whip yourself on the buttocks for as long as it takes you to recite the 'Salve Regina' (or 'Hail Holy Queen') hymn prayer. I have to say that I would recite the 'Salve Regina' as fast as I possibly could, because the whippings on such a delicate part of the body would peel the skin off and leave the flesh bare, no matter how fast you were when reciting your prayer.

BRAINWASHING

At the same time as members are taught to practise the techniques of mortification of the body, another more subtle and non-material practice takes place; this is no less important a formative task though than corporal self-punishment: the often mentioned 'brainwashing' technique, which is just a sophisticated method of psychological mortification that allows the order to manipulate people into converting.

The recruitment of new members constitutes what has been termed as 'sectarian proselytising'. Both young people and adults, especially those who are lacking in solid psychological bases, are easy prey to these types of methods, which generally consist of a dangerous mixture of affection and the imposition of a feeling of guilt. Brainwashing commonly begins with a positive dialogue that, gradually and almost unnoticeably, takes on the characteristics of what is really mental control; this is achieved through the use of techniques that change the individual's conduct. From the first moment in which youths enter the order's ranks, a male or female tutor is in charge of collecting information regarding their family lives: what is their parents' relationship like, do they go to mass, etc. Once a week, a sermon takes place (generally headed by the resident priest, but it can also be given by a male or female tutor) where a particular topic is made the object of guilt: divorce, premarital sex, etc. The director of the residence holds individual chats with the new recruits and in this way promotes a psychological dependency on this sort of conversations, the object of which is to trigger a vocational crisis in the young person.

Isolation plays a fundamental role during this stage in the recruitment process. By eliminating access to external information and influence (such as family, the media, etc.), The Work removes anything that could break up the process of assimilating feelings, attitudes and patterns of conduct that it is trying to impose on the new recruit. It is the practice of isolation that makes possible the integration of their sectarian ideas. In what way is this isolation achieved though? There are various ways. Spiritual retreats are one of the most common and effective; this is because the aspiring member remains in silence for several days, having to listen attentively to the talks and seminars given at a residence or isolated chalet. On the other hand, a very strict censorship is exerted regarding the books that the aspiring candidate is allowed to read. Colm Larkin, an ex-numerary of Irish origin, explains how every book that could be read by Opus Dei members carried a censorship rating that went from one to six. Those books that were rated with a number one could be read by everybody, while in order to read a book belonging to class number two members were forced to ask for permission. Those books rated between numbers three to five could only be read by established members and also depended on the years that they had belonged to The Work. Lastly, those books marked with a number six rating were completely banned to everybody, both to new candidates and to established members. Yet, perhaps the most influential form of isolation and of external influence control to which aspiring candidates are subjected is that of the control of their letters; that is, all letters are opened and read before they are handed over.

Subsequently, the recruitment process goes on to destroy the young candidate's ego and to diminish his or her personality, so that it does not interfere with or become dangerous to the psychological development of the whole group. The aim is to destroy the neophyte's original personality, so as to 'create' a new one for him or her, which is more useful to the function and objectives of The Work. In order to achieve this, and taking into account that all individuals are constituted by a psycho-physical unity, the process begins by coercing new entrants to despise their own body, since despising the body is a good starting point in the path to total self-loathing. And of course, within these feelings of aversion towards one's own material body, special emphasis is placed against anything related to sexuality and eroticism, which are clearly and unquestionably classified as a 'mortal sin'. The young initiate starts by hating his or her own body and viewing it as an enemy, something untrustworthy. The entrant then goes on to experience the same sort of feelings for him or herself, which in its turn leads him to put the trust he once had in himself on his director-instructor instead. Obviously, as the entrant's personality has been so completely dissolved at this stage, the trust he deposits in his superior is now total and absolute. It is at this stage when different types of corporal mortification start to be practised by the novice, including the ones we mentioned earlier (the use of the cilice and the discipline, etc.). The neophyte gladly accepts all of these in order to achieve the kind of salvation that he has heard so much about by now from his tutors, and also out of a need to 'please' and be liked by his superiors and the other members of the organization.

Additionally and in a parallel manner, all kinds of tactics are employed by the order so as to alter the novice's conscience and to produce intellectual disturbances in him or her. This method interrupts the novice's natural thinking process, and it is achieved by constant and repetitive indoctrination (for example, the same message is repeated over and over again, almost an infinite number of times), the use of set phrases and clichés that are easy to comprehend and to remember, etc. During this stage in the indoctrination process, it is fundamental that the neophyte is kept constantly occupied, and that someone accompanies him or her at all times.

When the novice has reached this point within the indoctrination process, he has been isolated, flagellated in both body and soul, bombarded with messages, has been continually active and never alone, so very little is left of his original individuality and freedom of thought. Constant employment and the fatigue that this carries with it, as well as bodily and psychological suffering, make it practically impossible for the novice to think or discern anything by him or herself. Physical weariness and the lack of sleep lead him, inevitably, to a weakening of his intellectual faculties and of his will.

He is now a worthy member of the Work of God.

BEYOND
THE DA
VINCI
CODE

GLOSSARY

GLOSSARY

This glossary has been compiled using the following criteria:

• Some of its words form part of the main body of this book and have not been fully developed within it, so that the glossary elaborates on them (for example, Asmodeus, the Sol Invictus, etc.).
• On the other hand, some words appear with very brief entries in this section, as they have been sufficiently expanded on within the main body of the book (for example, the cult of the Goddess, Mary Magdalene, the Merovingians, etc.).
• Lastly, this glossary also includes terms that do not appear within the present book, but that do make a brief appearance in *The Da Vinci Code* and are therefore developed and amplified within this section (for example, the Hebrew alphabet, Tarot cards, etc.).

A representation of
Asmodeus.

Asmodeus: one of the most powerful demons in existence, as he is supposed to hold seventy-two infernal legions under his command. According to the book of Tobias, he is also believed to be the instigator of base and carnal pleasures. He is said to have been the serpent that tempted Eve and so he is therefore portrayed with a serpent's tail. In the representation of his image we may also find the following satanic symbols: three heads – bull, man, and ram– and the feet of a crow, and he is usually portrayed riding a dragon. The work of this demon on earth is ambiguous: as well as being the ruler of pleasure, he is supposed to be linked to geometry, astronomy, and hidden treasures. According to legend, he assisted King Solomon in the construction of his temple. The Priory of Sion's secret dossiers refer to him as a 'guardian demon', and the Cathars worshipped him as the 'King of the World'.

Atbash code: Hebrew code that uses inverted writing, whereby the first letter of the alphabet is substituted with the last, the second letter with the one before last, and so on. It dates back to approximately 500 BC. Its use is to be found in the Kabbalah, in some of the Dead Sea scrolls, and in the Old Testament. It is also believed that the Knights Templar used it to code their secret messages.

Baphomet: a pagan demonic idol. The Knights Templar were accused of worshipping him.

Castelgandolfo: the Pope's summer residence situated on the borders of Lake Albano, thirty kilometres from the city of

Rome. From the times of Pope Urbane VIII, it has been established as a tradition that the Pope should spend his summer holidays at the castle. Its construction dates back to the 16th century, and it is the home of the Specula Vaticana, the papal astronomical observatory. It also possesses some wonderful gardens.

The entrance to Castelgandolfo.

Cathars: these were the supposed true descendants of the early Christians who settled in Western Europe, particularly within the region of Occitaine, in Southern France. They were also known by the name of Albigenses (from the famous city of Albi). The name 'Cathars' comes from the Greek word for 'pure', and they received this name from the Catholics. They called themselves 'good Christians' or 'good men'. Catharism was a philosophy that rekindled the most human concepts of early Christianity, and whose most revered text was the Gospel of St John. One of the most important duties and central aims of the Cathar lifestyle was the literal observation of the precepts of Jesus Christ, especially the ones that he offered at the Sermon on the Mount. The Cathars were characterized by a complete refusal of violence, lies and taking oaths. They presented themselves among Christian communities as preachers of the Word of God (itinerant and individually poor). The Cathar doctrine taught a dualistic vision of the universe where there existed two antagonistic principles: Good and Evil. They attributed the creation of the material world to the principle of Evil, and so they believed that everything that belonged to the physical world held negative and sinful characteristics. The only way to salvation was to follow the teachings of Jesus Christ,

The persecution of the Cathars during the times of the Inquisition.

who had showed to the world the road to redemption. They were totally against wars and the killing of animals, and they did not recognise the authority of kings, bishops, or the Pope. With their actions and beliefs, the Cathars managed to dissolve all of the existing priesthood within the Languedoc region, as they did not agree with the temporal power of the Church. For obvious reasons, none of their doctrine and teachings was well received by the Church in Rome, and so exhaustive efforts were made by the clergy in order to convert the Cathars to the orthodox beliefs of Catholicism. This was never achieved; on the contrary, the Cathars gained a growing number of adherents. The Church then tried to use its religious orders so as to influence them, but neither the Dominican Order nor the Cistercian Order was able to do this. The murder of Peter of Castlenou (the papal legate) in 1208 in mysterious circumstances, allowed Pope Innocent III to change his tactics and to use violence against the Cathars instead. In this way, what was a true crusade started against them. On the other hand, this situation offered the monarchy from the north of France a great opportunity to occupy the lands of the south, which were wealthier. Due to this, the Church was able to gain followers who helped in the extermination of the Cathar movement. Violence against the Cathars would continue later on, with the persecution and liquidation methods employed by the Inquisition.

Church of Saint Sulpice: Parisian church originally constructed by the Merovingian monarchy. It possesses a floor plan that is practically identical to that of the Cathedral of Notre Dame. The Priory of Sion has confirmed that this church was built on top of the ruins of an ancient temple, dedicated to the worship of Egyptian goddess Isis.

Clef de voute: secret technique used for the construction of domed arches (literally, 'key to the vault').

Cross: a symbol of death and redemption for Christians. However, the cross possessed a profound significance for diverse civilizations before Christianity. Among the people of Gaul, it was believed to hold fertility powers; for the people of Persia, it was a talisman against evil and death; in the religion of ancient Syria, it was an instrument of sacrifice to Baal, etc. Even to this date, crosses of different kinds are used as amulets and charms. The shape of the cross may be interpreted in two different ways: it can be read as the perpendicular intersection of two lines, or as the point from which four liines depart in four different directions. Due to these two different readings, the cross can be considered a symbol of conjunction or of inversion. Its vertical line symbolizes the positive principle, the axis of the world, spiritual elevation and the spiritual element while its transversal line symbolizes the negative principle, the order and the subjection of the world. Because of these two symbolic meanings, the cross also represents the moment when life and death approach each other, a meaning that becomes clear in the case of the Cross of Jesus Christ. It was mostly the Syrians who spread the use of the Christian cross during the first centuries of our own era; although it was not well accepted at the beginning, it

The cross is a symbol that has been transferred along different civilizations.

became used in a progressive manner. The reason for Christians' initial antagonism towards it was that the cross constituted the most shameful instrument of torture and ignominy, and so it was initially too terrible for them to accept it as a symbol of their God. Only after several centuries had gone by was the cross accepted by Christianity as its most important symbol. According to tradition, the authentic Cross of Christ was made out of olive tree, cypress, cedar, and palm wood, and its four arms represented the four sides of the world, the four seasons in a year and the four winds.

Cryptex: portable receptacle designed by Leonardo da Vinci to store any type of document (letters, maps, diagrams, etc.) in such a manner that the information remains sealed inside, within the container, and it can only be accessed by the person or persons who know the relevant code.

Cults of the Goddess: religious forms of a matriarchal order that were followed in antiquity. Within the majority of these religions, female sexuality, the moment of conception, the moment of birth and the idea of the earth understood as a womb were all fundamental concepts. In contrast to cults of a patriarchal order, the cult of the Goddess was generally exempt from cruelty.

Dead Sea scrolls: a collection of approximately six hundred manuscripts written in the Hebrew and Aramaic languages. They were discovered from 1946 onwards within a series of caves in present day Jordan, in the north-western region of the Dead Sea, within the province of Qirbet Qumran. Because of this, they are also

An image of the Mother Goddess holding a horn, which symbolizes abundance and the act of receiving. Museum of Aquitaine, Bordeaux, France.

A fragment from one of the Dead Sea scrolls.

known as the Qumran manuscripts. These writings form part of the Apocryphal Gospels, that is, those gospels that were not included within the orthodox Christian canon.

Fibonacci sequence: a mathematical progression in which each number is obtained through the sum of the two previous numbers. The mathematician Leonardo Fibonacci created it during the 13th century. It has been regarded as a sort of metaphor for the human condition, which helped to obtain a much deeper understanding and knowledge regarding the nature of spirituality.

The Fleur de lis.

Fleur de lis: a lily of the valley or iris flower, this is a plant with great symbolism. It has been given connotations of light, purity, life, and perfection. Also, it has been traditionally used to represent the French nobility, and was part of the armorial emblem of the kings of France. One of its many legends tells of how an angel offered the Merovingian King Clovis I a gold iris as a symbol of his purification when he converted to Christianity. Another legend explains how King Clovis accepted the flower as a royal symbol when some water lilies showed him the way to cross the river and win a battle. During the 14th century, the lily flower was often incorporated in the emblems of French noble families, and was sown into the cloak of a knight (worn over his body armour). The original aim of doing this was to identify different warriors during a battle, yet it developed in its turn into a system for the designation of social status. The Catholic Church uses the lily flower as a special emblem for the Virgin Mary and,

The Fleur de lis is used as a representation of the Virgin Mary and of the Holy Trinity.

The God Mithra.

because of its three petals, it is also used to represent the Holy Trinity.

God Mithra: also known as Mithras, this was a Persian deity who was also worshipped across the whole of the Roman Empire. In reality, Mithra was a human being who was made divine, and who is thought to have been born in 386 BC in Pontus, somewhere in Asia. Under the title of Mithra I, he was the governor of those regions until he was able to form his own empire. His successor, Mithra II, was defeated by the troops of Alexander the Great, and had to hand over the lands that he possessed. In the same line of succession, there were five more kings called Mithra: the seventh Mithra was known as Mithra the Great. It is a possibility that, in the first instance, Mithra could have travelled to the different regions on the borders of his own empire, leaving a legate behind in his place. When he returned to Persia, he could have then taken on the title of Mithra II, as if he were his own successor. Although there were constant wars assailing his people, King Mithra tried to find a harmonious relationship between his own spirit and that of God. He was successful in this aim, and, little by little, his internal equilibrium began to reflect itself in his exterior surroundings, as a consequence of the goodness of his soul. In this way, a series of mysteries and legends emerged in relation to his person. His legend gradually grew in importance, until King Mithra became the most important of Persian gods, the personification of light in the world, and therefore the enemy of evil and of darkness. He was believed to be the son of the God of the Sun, and it was said that he had been born in a cave or cavern during the winter solstice. The celebrations in his honour were exuberant and extensive, and would take place within subterranean passageways during the shortest day of the year. In addition, daily rituals in his honour took place, during which hymns were sung at an altar constructed on top of mount Pyraethea; at this altar, and protected by some sort of cell, burned The Eternal Fire. The mysteries of Mithra celebrated in this manner spread throughout all of Mesopotamia, until they arrived in Rome and were gradually propagated across the entire Roman Empire. All of the monuments that were constructed in his honour had seven altars or pyres consecrated to the seven planets, which the ancient Persians knew very well. The caves in which he was worshipped were therefore true 'planetaria', as they presented the totality of the known Cosmos, including its planets, their orbits around the sun, and their respective distances and sizes. Finally, around the 4th century, Mithraism – the name of the religion originating from the cult to this god – faded, as many other pagan cults did with the advance of Christianity. Many of its followers were converted to the Christian religion, while others decided to follow the sect of the Manicheans.

Hebrew Alphabet: Hebrew is a Semitic language originally adopted by the Ibri or Israelites when they took possession of the land of Canaan, to the West of the river Jordan in Palestine. Its letters, in addition to possessing a very beautiful form, carry profound meaning, not only in their individual state but also in the different combinations that give form to words. Furthermore, each individual letter holds a

ا ب پ ت ث ج ح خ
ظ ع غ ف ق ك ك ل
١ ٢ ٣ ٤ ٥ ٦ ٧ ٨ ٩ ٠

ا ب پ ت ث ج ح خ
ظ ع غ ف ق ك ك ل
١ ٢ ٣ ٤ ٥ ٦ ٧ ٨ ٩ ٠

ا ب پ ت ث ج ح خ
ظ ع غ ف ق ك ك ل
١ ٢ ٣ ٤ ٥ ٦ ٧ ٨ ٩ ٠

The Hebrew alphabet is a Semitic language originally adopted by the Israelites

135

The letters of the Hebrew alphabet are filled with a profound meaning. This meaning is not only contained within each individual letter, but also appears in the combination of these when forming words.

numerical value, which helps cabbalists to perform diverse interpretations and readings. What follows is a brief synopsis of each of the letters of the Hebrew alphabet, including their numerical values and individual meanings:

Aleph: this is the first letter of the alphabet. Its arithmetic value is one, and it symbolizes the divine penetrating force that was experienced during the act of creation, when the birth of the different existing letters took place.

Bet: this is the second letter, with a numerical value of two. It corresponds to the second day of Genesis, when God separated the upper waters from the lower ones.

Gimel: this is the third letter, with a value of three. It is the symbol representing the movement of man along the path of his life, from his conception to his ultimate decay.

Dalet: this is the fourth letter, with a value of four. It is the symbol for pausing, trials, and prison.

He: this is the fifth letter, with an arithmetic value of five. It symbolizes life expressed through the act of breathing.

Waw: this is the sixth letter, with a value of six. It represents something that has been completed and finished, just as the world was created in six days.

Zayin: this is the seventh letter, with a value of seven. It symbolises spiritual values, which are the most important thing in this world.

Het: this is the eighth letter, with a value of eight. It represents mankind's potential ability to pass beyond the limits of this world. On the other hand, it also symbolizes sin, as well as purification.

Tet: this is the ninth letter, with a value of nine. It expresses the absolute perfection involved in creation. It also symbolizes the protection offered by the divine.

Yod: this is the tenth letter, with a value of ten. It is connected to the word 'yad' (which means 'hand') and symbolizes the action and the power of creation.

Kaph: this is the eleventh letter, with a numerical value of twenty. It symbolizes the 'Kether' or crown.

Lamed: this is the twelfth letter, with a numerical value of thirty. Its name means 'to teach, to instruct, to learn'.

Mem: this is the thirteenth letter, with a value of forty. Basically, it is a symbol for the female womb and for the primordial waters.

Nun: this is the fourteenth letter, with a value of fifty. It is intimately linked to unity and totality.

Samekh: this is the fifteenth letter of the Hebrea alphabet, with an arithmetic value of sixty. For Hebrews, it represents Tradition and points at the concept of divine assistance.

Ayin: this is the sixteenth letter, with a value of seventy. It marks the concealment that is a necessary part of any search whose goal is to conquer light. It also symbolizes understanding, and internal vision.

Pe: this is the seventeenth letter, with a numerical value of eighty. Its name comes from the word 'peh' (which means 'mouth'), and therefore it is a symbol for openings and the word.

Tsade: this is the eighteenth letter, with a value of ninety. Its ancient ideogram symbolizes the head of a harpoon.

Qoph: this is the nineteenth letter, with a value of one hundred. It indicates and symbolizes divine sanctity.

A representation of the Hieros Gamos ritual.

Res: this is the twentieth letter, with a numerical value of two hundred. It refers to the beginning, to the head and to the most important things.

Sin: this is the twenty-first letter, with a value of three hundred. Its symbol is a reserve of energy that contains a cosmic explosion.

Taw: this is the twenty-second letter, with a value of four hundred. It is the same as the word 'taw', which means 'mark' or 'signal'.

Hierodules: priestesses consecrated to the cult of the Goddess, who celebrated the mystery of carnal love not as a formalist and symbolic ritual, but as a magical and purposeful ceremony. This ceremony took place in order to feed the psychic current that gave a physical body to the presence of the Goddess, while, at the same time, to transmit to those who were united with the hierodules the influence or virtue of that deity, as in a sacrament. It was believed that the hierodules embodied the Goddess in a certain form, that they were the 'carriers' of the female deity. During these rituals, the sexual act held, on the one hand, the general function that evocative sacrifices or rituals capable of bringing to life divine entities had; on the other hand, it had a role structurally identical to that of the presence of the Eucharist: it was, for the man, the means to participate in the sacrament, led and administrated by the female. It was, basically, a technique to achieve contact with the deity and to open to her through the interruption of the ordinary and of individual self-realization that the sexual act normally carries with it. The hierodules have also often been known, in a rather deprecatory manner, as 'sacred prostitutes'.

Hieros Gamos: a sacred matrimony ritual that dates back to ancient Sumeria. During this ritual, the Goddess is embodied by the high priestess. She practised the sexual act with the governor of the country in order to show the Goddess' acceptance of him as the protector of the land. Later on, and in a more all-encompassing manner, hieros gamos was considered to be the ritual union of a man and a woman destined to celebrate and renew the mystery of the union between the eternal masculine and the eternal feminine, of the heavens with the earth. It was believed that the individuals who performed these rituals embodied their corresponding principles and that their momentary physical union would be transformed into an evocative reconstruction of the divine union that was beyond time and space.

Holy Grail: a mysterious object that, throughout history, has been said to own a multiplicity of material shapes as well as of symbolic meanings. Among these are: the cup from which Jesus Christ and his disciples drank during the Last Supper, the

A Templar knight kneeling in front of the Holy Grail.

chalice in which Joseph of Arimathea collected the blood of Christ on the Cross, etc. *The Da Vinci Code* adheres to the theory that the Holy Grail was the receptacle that collected and contained the blood (in the sense of 'lineage' or 'bloodline') of Jesus Christ, that is, the womb of Mary Magdalene and, by extension, Mary Magdalene herself.

Isis: Female Egyptian deity. She was the most powerful goddess of ancient Egypt and was linked to maternity and fertility.

King Arthur: a legendary British monarch (although a few scholars have placed him in France). He is the utmost hero of the so-called Arthurian cycle. His personality is strongly identified with the occult because of his mysterious origins, the further enigmatic events in his lifetime and the fact that his court was a centre for more or less supernatural phenomena. According to

Isis, the goddess of Egyptian mysteries.

According to legend, King Arthur and his queen were buried at Glastonbury Abbey.

tradition, he lived during the first half of the 6th century AD, and was educated by Merlin the sorcerer, one of the greatest and best known esoteric names of primitive times. Merlin initiated Arthur into the secret doctrine and the mysteries of natural magic; he also helped him to become a military general. When he was crowned king at the age of fifteen, King Arthur founded the Order of the Knights of the Round Table. Both King Arthur and the order that he created are linked to the enigma of the Holy Grail.

The mythical King Arthur in a painting from his era.

Leicester codex: a book of notes written by Leonardo da Vinci between 1506 and 1510 when he was at Milan. It consists of seventy-two pages, and contains brilliant scientific notes and excellent deductions. It received its name from the English family that acquired it in the year 1717. It is to be found today in the hands of Bill Gates, co-founder of Microsoft and the richest man in the world.

Louvre museum: this wonderful museum is situated in Paris, and was founded in 1793. Its collections are organized into seven different departments, and they include artworks ranging from the birth of the world's greatest civilizations, to the second half of the 19th century. Within these collections we may find works by celebrated painters such as Rembrandt, Titian and Rubens, as well as one of the most famous sculptures in the entire world: the Venus de Milo. The museum also contains and imposing collection of ancient Greek and Roman antiquities, as well as a department solely dedicated to artefacts from ancient Egypt.

The Louvre museum.

141

The book cover of *Malleus Maleficarum*. Written in 1486 by Dominican monks, this handbook for the persecution of witches and sorcerers was used for two centuries by both Catholics and Protestants.

Malleus Maleficarum: also known as 'the hammer of sorcerers'. This was a book dating back to the Middle Ages that was used by the Inquisition to detect and battle against witchcraft. Its authors were Jakob Sprenger and Heinrich Kramer, two Dominican monks who were employed as inquisitors with special powers. Pope Innocent II passed a bull by which they were charged with investigating crimes of witchcraft in northern Germany. This famous witch-hunting handbook dates back to 1486, and more than thirty editions of it were published during the two years that followed its original publication. Although further handbooks on similar subject-matter were issued subsequently (such as the *Compendium Maleficarum*), these were mostly just simple paraphrases of the original title. Within their book, Spranger and Kramer emphasize that witchcraft is a phenomenon that is essentially female, and with this statement they express the ancient sentiment of misogyny and the mistrust felt by the Church towards women; according to this institution, the daughters of Eve constitute the focus of eternal temptation. One the book's passages states regarding women that 'their face is like a wind that burns the skin, their voice is like the sibilant whistling of a serpent that can place curses on a multitude of animals and human beings.' The fear of female sexuality is also present in the book; its passages referring to women reveal the fear and hostility professed by these two Dominican monks towards the fairer sex, although their stance was in fact rather a common one within the Church at the time.

The book is divided into three parts. The first part is essentially dedicated to revealing the reality and danger of witchcraft. Within the second part, three different classes of witches are described and defined: those who make people sick and can also cure them, those who are only able to make people ill, and those who are able only to heal them. Therefore, according to the latter category, any female healer could be accused of being an accomplice to the Devil. This part of the book also recommends a series of defensive methods against curses. Lastly, the third part of the books constitute a sort of guide on how to conduct a judiciary process against a sorcerer or a witch. Within this part, the book's authors argue the acceptability of using torture methods in the process.

One of the codices belonging to the Nag Hammadi manuscript collection.

Manuscripts of Nag Hammadi: a compilation of codices found in Egypt in 1945. They contain a series of Gnostic works, which form a large part of what are known as the Apocryphal Gospels, those that were discarded during the construction of a canonical or official version of the Bible.

Contents:

– Codex I (also known as *The Jung Foundation Codex*):
> • *The Prayer of the Apostle Paul*
> • *The Apocryphon of James* (also known as *The Secret Book of James*)
> • *The Gospel of Truth*
> • *The Treatise on the Resurrection*
> • *The Tripartite Tractate*

– Codex II:
> • The Apocryphon of John
> • *The Gospel of Thomas* – a gospel of sayings

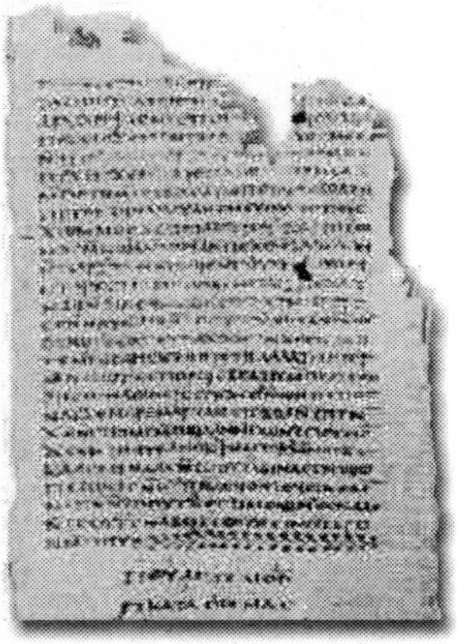

One of the codices belonging to the Nag Hammadi manuscript collection.

- *The Gospel of Philip* – a gospel of sayings
- *The Hypostasis of the Archons*
- *On the Origin of the World*
- *The Exegesis on the Soul*
- *The Book of Thomas the Contender*

– Codex III:
- *The Apocryphon of John*
- *The Gospel of the Egyptians*
- *Eugnostos the Blessed*
- *The Sophia of Jesus Christ*
- *The Dialogue of the Saviour*

– Codex IV:
- *The Apocryphon of John*
- *The Gospel of the Egyptians*

– Codex V:
- *Eugnostos the Blessed*
- *The Apocalypse of Paul*
- *The First Apocalypse of James*
- *The Second Apocalypse of James*
- *The Apocalypse of Adam*

– Codex VI:
- *The Acts of Peter and the Twelve Apostles*
- *The Thunder, Perfect Mind*
- *Authoritative Teaching*
- *The Concept of Our Great Power*
- Plato's *Republic* – the original is not Gnostic, but the Nag Hammadi library version is heavily modified with current Gnostic concepts.
- *The Discourse on the Eighth and Ninth* – a Hermetic treatise
- *The Prayer of Thanksgiving* (with a hand-written note) – a Hermetic prayer
- Fragment from *Asclepius* (21-29) – another Hermetic treatise

– Codex VII:
- *The Paraphrase of Shem*

144

- *The Second Treatise of the Great Seth*
- *Apocalypse of Peter*
- *The Teachings of Silvanus*
- *The Three Steles of Seth*
– Codex VIII:
  - *Zostrianos*
  - *The Letter of Peter to Philip*
– Codex IX:
  - *Melchizedek*
  - *The Thought of Norea*
  - *The Testimony of Truth*
– Codex X:
  - *Marsanes*
– Codex XI:
  - *The Interpretation of Knowledge*
  - *A Valentinian Exposition, On the Anointing, On Baptism* (A and B) and *On the Eucharist* (A and B)
  - *Revelations received by Allogenes*
  - *Hypsiphrone*
– Codex XII
  - *The Sentences of Sextus*
  - Central fragment from *the Gospel of Truth*
  - Unidentified fragments
– Codex XIII:
  - *The Trimorphic Protennoia*
  - *On the Origin of the World*

Mary Magdalene, the wife of Jesus Christ.

Mary Magdalene: a descendant of the tribe of Benjamin. She was the wife of Jesus Christ and the mother of their daughter Sarah.

Merovingians: the first and mythical Frankish dynasty existing during the Middle Ages. They were the descendants of Jesus Christ.

145

A pentacle.

Mystery of Sheshach: 'Sheshach' is the same as the city of 'Babel'; the city's name is written using the Atbash code. The word 'mystery' refers to the fact that, for many years, researchers and scholars remained confused regarding Biblical references to a city named Sheshach. When they applied the Atbash code to these, it became evident that the name of Shehach was in fact referring to the name of the city of Babel.

Number Phi: 1.618. This number is derived from the Fibonacci sequence and it possesses a fundamental role as the basic mould for all of Nature's creations. For example, Phi is the result of the difference between the diameters of every section of a nautilus' spiral shell, it also constitutes the number of spirals that form pine cones, etc. Because of this series of numerical coincidences, ancient scholars believed that the Creator of the Universe had predetermined the number Phi, and early scientists baptized it with the name of 'the divine proportion'. For numerous artists, the number Phi represented the maximum expression of beauty, the perfect proportion; hence, this is the reason why it appears within a large number of buildings and works of art, from antiquity to the present times. Examples of famous constructions that have used the number Phi are the Parthenon and the pyramid of Keops.

Pentacle: this star with five points has been given several different names by esoteric doctrine: pentacle, pentagram, pentalf, and – curiously – witch's foot. This symbol constitutes the geometrical representation of the number five, and it also synthesizes the union of unequal entities. It is a cosmos

146

of small proportions, since it adds up the masculine and the feminine principles. As mentioned in *The Da Vinci Code*, it is a pre-Christian symbol related to the cult of nature and the world, and it is conceived in terms of the masculine and the feminine. It appears that it has its origins in ancient Egypt, where it was read as the representation of the god Horus, who personified the universal seed of all beings, the primal matter from which all of humanity had been created. The followers of Greek mathematician Pythagoras used the pentacle symbol as a way of recognizing each other. Early Christians also used to employ it as an emblem, prior to adopting the symbol of the cross. Paracelsus, the famous alchemist and medical doctor based in Basel (Switzerland), considered the pentacle to be one of the most potent of symbolic formulas; due to this, occultism transformed this graphic representation of Pythagorean knowledge into a symbol of the path to magic. Within rituals and magic spells, it can be used to symbolize either the forces of Good or the forces of Evil. When only one of its vertices is placed pointing upwards, it can suggest the shape of the human body (the head, the arms and the legs spread out), and it is used as such in white magic or theurgical practices. This representation of the pentacle reflects the active equilibrium and the capacity of understanding needed by man in order to create for himself a centre of life irradiating its own light. The portrayal of a man within this geometrical figure (see: Vitruvian Man) is a synonym for the canon of aesthetics, a symbol of beauty and the secret of the divine proportion. When the pentacle figure is inverted, the two upper vertices form a

The pentacle symbolises the figure of a man with arms and legs outspread. Its five points represent the spirit, air, fire, water and earth. For Christians, these same five points symbolize the five wounds of Jesus. It is one of the symbols most preferred by sorcerers, as it holds the power to drive away evil spirits and to attract good fortune. However, when inverted it represents the Devil's goat and the foot of a witch.

similar shape to that of the horns of the
Devil, and it used as such in black magic.
Among Freemasons, the pentacle was called
the Shining Star, and constituted the
emblem for the power of genius, which
elevates the soul in order to achieve grand
goals. It is believed that it is because of
Masonry that the star with five points forms
part of the emblems belonging to the USA,
Russia, and several countries situated in the
Middle East.

Q document: a book containing some of
the teachings of Jesus Christ that – it is
presumed – could have been written by
Jesus himself.

Rose: the rose is one of the most important
and complex of esoteric symbols. It
constitutes an ambivalent symbol as, on the
one hand, a white rose represents purity,
innocence, and virginity, while a red rose
refers to the contrary: carnal passion and
fertility. This flower also represents time and
eternity and life and death. In addition, it
personifies the image of mystery; the heart
of the rose implies the unknown, while the
whole of the flower indicates plenitude.
When used to reflect life, it is portrayed as a
symbol of spring, resurrection, love and
fertility. If it is used to portray death, it is
presented as a symbol for the temporal and
for pain. On the other hand, roses, wine,
sensuality and seduction have always
constituted a sort of inseparable quartet. Its
thorns also link the rose to pain, blood and
martyrdom. A red rose was used to
symbolize the king, the sun, gold, and fire;
on the other hand, a white rose was
employed to represent the queen, the moon,
silver and water. Red and white roses put

together represent death, but in the sense of
the final integration with the One, with
whom the individual self is merged in order
to live again. A gold rose has always
symbolized perfection, while a blue rose
represented the impossible. In alchemy, the
rose represented wisdom. It has also been
used as an esoteric symbol by different
orders belonging to that field of study as a
kind of emblem (as, for example, the
Rosicrucians). Within Christian tradition, a
red rose can constitute a symbol for the
Virgin Mother or for the blood spilled by
Christ when he was on the Cross. In *The Da
Vinci Code*, this flower is also linked to the
pentacle (a star with five points), as both
constitute symbols of femininity.
Furthermore, a rose with five petals is the
symbol adopted by the Priory of Sion to
portray the Holy Grail.

The emblem of the
Enlightened Rosicrucians.

Rose line: a sort of ancient Greenwich
meridian line, this was the first zero
longitude in the world. It consisted of an
imaginary line traced from the North to the
South Pole. It was used as a way of
measuring all of the other terrestrial
longitudinal lines. It runs across the Church
of Saint Sulpice in Paris.

Rosicrucians: during the second decade of
the 17th century, a series of strange
documents appeared in Germany. The
uncovered texts revealed the existence of a
secret brotherhood founded during the 15th
century by somebody named Christian
Rosencreutz, and whose followers formed
part of a secret fraternity or guild of mystic
initiates. The text in question was titled *The
Chymical Wedding of Christian Rosencreutz*
('the Christian of the cross of roses') and its

author was Johannes Valentinus Andreae, one of the Priory of Sion's Grand Masters. This work had an evidently satirical intent, and its objective was to ridicule the many impostors wanting to pass as true alchemists. Yet, the truth is that it caused a sensational stir throughout the whole of Europe: important members of the occultist world tried to get in touch with the 'Rosicrucians' in order to join their order; meanwhile, others proclaimed that they had already been in contact with these mysterious wise men for some time. Since then, the legend of the Rosicrucians has continued to fascinate occultist followers throughout the Western world. At present, numerous societies purport to be Rosicrucians or state that they are in possession of the secret doctrines of Christian Rosencreutz.

Rosslyn Chapel: also known as the 'Cathedral of Enigmas'. This is a church situated in Scotland, about ten kilometres from Edinburgh. Rosslyn Chapel contains a

(Left) The Masonic ceremony of the Cross of the Rose. (Right) The symbol of the Brotherhood of the Cross of the Rose.

large number of Christian symbols, as well as Masonic, Egyptian, pagan, and Hebrew symbols. Contrary to popular thought, it was not constructed by the Knights Templar, but by Sir William St Clair during the 15th century, when the Knights Templar had already been extinct for a century.

Secret dossiers: secret archives belonging to the Priory of Sion that were found at the National Library of Paris. They contain the history of the Priory, a list of its Grand Masters, newspapers cuttings, letters and genealogies including, among others, that of the descendants of Jesus Christ and Mary Magdalene.

Shekinah: the female equivalent of God. According to the early Jewish people, she was housed within the Temple of Solomon by the side of her male counterpart. Within Gnostic thought, Shekinah is the human soul in exile. She presents a double enigma, and within the Old Testament she is the shining cloud mentioned in rabbinical texts, which was said to reside within the Ark of the Covenant, at the so-called Santa Sanctorum Church. She is also referred to within certain Biblical dictionaries as 'the name of God'; the veil of God that protects humanity from His terrifying presence, but which at the same time represents His compassion. Kabbalists personify Shekinah as a woman: she is the Sophia, the wisdom of God, the partner in the shadow of God or the stone of exile. Shekinah is also a well known figure in Islamic culture, especially within the esoteric tradition of Sufism, where she is known as Sakina.

The facade and interior of Rosslyn Chapel.

A representation of the Sol Invictus

Sol Invictus: a cult whose name literally means 'Invincible Sun'. This was a religious cult of Assyrian origin that was imposed by ancient Roman emperors on their subjects, a century before the reign of Constantine the Great. Because of its origins, the Sol Invictus cult included elements of the cults of Baal and Ashtarte. Nevertheless, it was a monotheistic cult in essence, and it represented the Sun God as the sum of all of the other Gods' attributes. In a parallel manner, it was similar to the cult of Mithra, which also existed in Rome during the same epoch, and which was equal to Sol Invictus in its profound adoration of the king of heavenly bodies.

Specula Vaticana: an astronomical observatory and research institution that forms part of the Holy See. It holds a specialist library that is believed to contain more than twenty-five thousand volumes; among these, we may find unique texts by authors such as Isaac Newton, Johannes Kepler, Nicholas Copernicus and Galileo Galilei.

The Star of David.

Star of David: also known as the seal of King Solomon, this is a hexagram formed by the superimposition of two triangles. Originally, it constituted the symbol for astronomical priests. Later on, the Israelite kings David and Solomon adopted it. The triangle pointing upwards can be interpreted as a sword (a primarily masculine symbol), and the inverted triangle as a chalice (which represents the female), and therefore the Star of David constitutes a symbol for the perfect union between man and woman.

Tarot cards: a set of seventy-eight playing cards. The pack is divided into two distinct sets, the Major Arcana and the Minor Arcana. The Minor Arcana set is formed by fifty-six cards, in its turn divided into four different suits: swords, batons, cups, and coins. The first two suits are of a masculine order. The batons (as well as constituting a phallic symbol) represent energy and action, while the swords (a phallic symbol too) refer to the power of the mind and its ideas. The cups and coins suits are linked to the feminine due to their shape (the coins are round, while the cups are recipients waiting to be filled), but also because of what they represent: the cups stand for affection, the subconscious and emotions, while the coins suit refers to the earth. The twenty-two remaining cards constitute the Major Arcana, and each one of them symbolises a scene in the search for spirituality. As it is mentioned within *The Da Vinci Code*, these remaining cards may be read as a sort of visual catechesis that explains the history of the lost Maiden and of how she was oppressed by the malevolent Church. The symbolism lying within the Major Arcana is as follows:

The Tarot cards employed by fortune tellers and sorcerers of all times.

The Magician: this is the first card in the pack. It symbolizes creativity, initiative, and the active principle. It is linked to the original cause, and to the origin of things.
The Popess or the High Priestess: this card is essentially tied to the female principle, and refers to fertility, realization, equilibrium and serenity. It is also a symbol for the sanctuary, knowledge, the law and women.
The Empress: this card constitutes another female archetype. It is a symbol for the spiritual, lucidity, fertility and the creation of

The Justice card.

the world. It presents the feminine influence of the woman that is loved, the wife, or the female friend.

The Emperor: this card constitutes the first male archetype in the pack. It symbolizes the law, strength, stability, legality, success and power.

The Hierophant or the Pope: this card represents the voice of conscience, moral authority and respect for traditions.

Justice: this card stands for equilibrium, equity, honesty, just recompense and merited punishment.

The Lovers: this card alludes to being united, enchantment, equilibrium and the act of sex. It also symbolizes the need for love and to choose freely.

The Chariot: this card speaks of triumph, independence, self-will and clearly defined dreams.

The Hermit: this card presents a male archetype symbolizing wisdom, Good, morality, the sense of duty, serenity and mental reflection.

The Wheel of Fortune: this card represents the spirit confronting its destiny, the inevitable transformations that occur along the process of life and fate affecting human destiny.

Strength: this card symbolizes the eternal spirit that is capable of triumphing over obstacles and resistance, the triumph of reason over instinct or of man over nature and intelligence that subjects brute force.

The Hanged Man: this card symbolizes the spirit of renunciation and sacrifice, passive mystical initiation, abnegation, the lack of interest in earthly matters and altruism. It is also a symbol for the Calvary, punishment and temporal limitations.

Death: this card does not refer specifically to

its name, but rather to a profound change that will allow rebirth and to the destruction and desolation from which life will be reborn. It is a symbol for radical transformation that promises rebirth; it also holds an intimate link with alchemical and esoteric matters.

The Tower: this card is a sign for alterations and weaknesses; it represents the spirit faced with destruction, strength and violence, the loss of stability, sudden and complete changes, dilapidation, the fall and collapse.

The Star: this card is, above all, a symbol for the luminosity that serves as a guide to lost humanity, but it is also linked to occult faculties, and to secret protections. It represents the spirit endowed with hope, the feeling of being protected by the universe, placing one's trust in one's own instincts and spiritual peace.

The Moon: this card is linked to intuition, the imagination, dreams and madness. It refers to uncertainty, fears, obstacles, the subconscious and memories.

The Sun: this card symbolizes the opposites that unite, the capacity to perceive things in a simple manner, the interior self that is liberated from fear, glory, spirituality and enlightenment, realization and success.

Judgement: this card symbolizes the moment of truth, the definitive trial at which each and everyone has to assume his or her own responsibilities. It also speaks of a flight towards spirituality performed with joy and full consciousness.

The World: a Goddess, with all that she implies, represents this card. She holds two sticks in her hands in order to capture the energies of the world. It speaks of realization, total victory, plenitude,

The Wheel of Fortune card.

The Temperance card.

happiness and of the spirit that has left the material world behind.

The Fool: In general terms, this card symbolizes travel, new experiences, spontaneity, enthusiasm and adventure. Its negative side implies madness, non-reflection, extravagance and a lack of discipline.

Temperance: this card represents the spirit having to contain itself, and it alludes to the patience that is necessary in order to make our dreams a reality. It also symbolizes healing, regeneration, transformation, serenity and spirituality.

The Devil: this card symbolizes 'the game of the Devil', or situations in which fiction and reality intermingle. It speaks of enchantment, magic, eloquence, and mystery.

Templar (or Maltese) cross: a red cross whose arms are wider at the ends than at their origins. It was adopted by the Knights of the Order of the Temple as their emblem, and it decorated the white cloak that constituted the habit of the Order.

Temple Church: this church is situated between the River Thames and Fleet Street in London. It was constructed during the 12th century by the Knights Templar, and was consecrated in the year 1185 by Emperor Heraclius, the patriarch of Jerusalem. The consecration took place during a ceremony that was attended – according to popular theory – by Henry II, King of England. Originally, as well as the temple, the church complex included accommodation for the knights, recreational areas and a space for military training. After 1307, when the Order of the Knights

Templar was dissolved, Edward II took possession of it and it became part of the monarchy's holdings. Later on, it was handed over to the Order of the Knights Hospitalers. Temple church is circular, and is based on the Church of the Holy Sepulchre in Jerusalem. In the past, it formed the setting for many famous passages in British history, and at present, it holds mass services on Sundays.

Vatican's secret archives: a collection of books, codices and scrolls that are stored at the Holy See, and which is not open to the general public.

Vitruvian Man: an artwork by Leonardo da Vinci that constitutes a vision of man as the centre of the universe. In order to show this, the Vitruvian man is contained within a circle and a square. The square forms the basis of classical art and proportion: its module is used in all classical architecture,

Temple Church in London, which houses a series of effigies of Crusader knights.

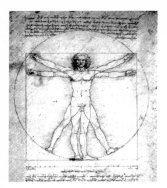

The Vitruvian Man, Leonardo da Vinci's portrayal of the perfect proportions of the human body.

while its 90° angles and its symmetrical form are the Greco-Roman basis of all architecture. With this drawing, da Vinci performed an anatomical study in search of the correct proportions of the human body, the classical canon or ideal of human beauty. Da Vinci followed the research done by architect Vitruvius (Marcus Vitruvius Pollio), a Roman architect who lived during the 1st century BC, and who was employed by Emperor Julius Caesar to construct war machines. Vitruvian Man constitutes a clear example of the globalizing perspective developed extremely rapidly by Leonardo da Vinci during the second half of the 1480s. Its aim is to link architecture and the human body: an aspect of da Vinci's interpretation of nature and of his vision of humanity's position within the 'global plan of things'.